RED GOLDFISH

NONPROFIT EDITION

HOW THE BEST NONPROFITS LEVERAGE THEIR PURPOSE TO INCREASE ENGAGEMENT AND IMPACT

Stan Phelps & Keith Green

© 2019 by Stan Phelps and Keith Green

All rights reserved. No part of this work covered by the copyright herein may be reproduced, transmitted, stored or used in any form including but not limited to photocopying, recording, scanning, digitizing, taping, web distribution, information networks, information storage or retrieval systems, except as permitted by Section 107 or 108 of the 1976 Copyright Act, without the prior written permission of the publisher.

Published by 9 INCH

Copy Editing by Lee Heinrich

Layout by Amit Dey

Special thanks to Jeanne Allen and Hope Freedman for their input

ISBN: 978-1-7326652-6-2

1. Nonprofit 2. Leadership 3. Purpose 4. Organizational Effectiveness

First Printing: 2019

Printed in the United States of America

Red Goldfish Nonprofit Edition is available for bulk orders. For further details and special pricing, please e-mail stan@purplegoldfish.com or call +1.919.360.4702.

This book is dedicated to my mother-in-law, Christina Wills. For the last 25 years she's been an integral member of the Thomas Merton Center, a nonprofit in Bridgeport, Connecticut. As a Case Manager/ Programs Supervisor, she is a tireless advocate, whether it's facilitating support groups, supervising the soup kitchen, interacting with guests, or coordinating with community service programs.

- Stan Phelps

This book is dedicated to my mom, Brenda, and my wife, Donna. Their impressive careers are highlighted by "giving back" through the teaching profession, which helped inspire me to start the Autism MVP Foundation, a nonprofit dedicated to increasing the number of autism-focused educators and therapists. This book is also dedicated to my late father, Dave, and my son, Gavin, who have inspired me in different but important ways to help me become the person I am today.

- Keith Green

FOREWORD

By
Lisa Bowman

"We make a living by what we get. We make a life by what we give."

- Winston Churchill

At one point or another, most of us stop and take a hard look at ourselves and wonder if there's more we should do to help others. For some, it's a sense of obligation, while others find joy in giving someone a leg up in life. Whatever your motivation, I firmly believe that the generosity of the human spirit is needed now more than ever.

Growing up in Chicago, I saw firsthand how much my parents enjoyed and thrived at their jobs –Dad owned an ad agency and Mom was a VP of Development at the March of Dimes. Inspired by their work ethic and driven by a sense of purpose, I studied marketing and spent the past 25 years creating relationships between brands, teams, individuals, and companies in various industry sectors. I spent the bulk of that time at UPS, building relationships with customers and ensuring their experience with the brand was positive and meaningful.

About 13 years ago, I was tapped by UPS to participate in a month-long community internship program in McAllen, TX. I stepped away from my daily office work and spent my time learning about the challenges facing the community and how best to address them. The experience was eye-opening and prompted me to take a hard look at my life. I'd always been quick to write a check for charity but now had the opportunity to see from a firsthand perspective what was happening on the ground in a community vastly different than mine. As a result, I was able to get engaged by "getting my hands dirty" to actually do the work, versus providing financial support from afar.

Soon after, I began working at The UPS Foundation where I oversaw the transportation company's annual United Way campaign. This gave me the unique opportunity to leverage my marketing skills to rally employees around a purpose to improve lives around the world. Through the simple act of positioning United Way as a product for purchase, with features and benefits, I was able to increase the campaign from $48 million to over $65 million in four years. When United Way needed a new chief marketing officer, I jumped at the chance to leverage the intersection of my professional power and personal purpose to further our shared goals of building stronger communities around the world.

As shared in *Red Goldfish Nonprofit Edition,* I've also seen how nonprofits and businesses share more in common than I previously thought. In the same way that companies are accountable to shareholders and investors, nonprofits must answer to their stakeholders – the board members, staff, donors and volunteers that invest their resources with us with the intent of generating a social return on investment.

As a nonprofit organization, we must be cognizant and appreciative of each and every "sale" we make – whether it's $20 million, $200 or 20 hours of volunteer time. We have to ensure a good experience that provides our stakeholders with a reason to "buy more" and recommend us to friends and family. This imperative is at the heart of *Red Goldfish Nonprofit Edition.*

Whether you are the largest privately-funded nonprofit in the world or the smallest nonprofit, we all have a unique platform to create expansive change. With that comes the great responsibility to continually deliver on our purpose and drive the engagement of our stakeholders. We owe them that. This book provides the I.D.E.A. framework that gives you the tools to bring your purpose to life.

Our work at United Way Worldwide is fueled by the passion of more than 3 million volunteers and nearly 10 million donors who through the power of our network speak up, unite, and take action on issues through giving, advocating, and volunteering.They're fighting with us to create a better world, and the best way we can support them is by honoring the trust they've instilled in us.

Lisa Bowman is the CMO of United Way Worldwide, the world's largest privately-funded nonprofit with 60,000 global partner companies. United Way has been living its purpose of bringing people together to build stronger communities for more than 130 years. Lisa was preciously both a board member and the board chair of United Way's Global Corporate Leaders Advisory Council. She was the American Marketing Association's 2017 Nonprofit Marketer of the Year and also holds a seat on the National Board of the AMA.

TABLE OF CONTENTS

INTRODUCTION

BY KEITH GREEN

"The two most important days in your life are the day you were born and the day you find out why."

– Mark Twain

It was June of 2009 and my wife, Donna, and I were terrified. We were visiting a neurologist's office for the second time in six months, and the doctor had just conducted a second round of field tests on our son. She then excused herself from her office for a few minutes, and after what seemed like an eternity, she reentered the room and closed the door.

What she said next changed our lives and our family's path in many ways. It was all such a blur. I don't recall her sentence verbatim—just that her findings were "consistent with autism."

Our two-year-old son, who was struggling to communicate and had missed a handful of traditional milestones, was now part of a frightening statistic. According to the Centers for Disease Control and Prevention (CDC), 1 in 59 children born today are on the autism spectrum. (When our son was born, that figure was 1 in 88).

What we did not know at the time was that there were brighter days ahead for our family—thanks to many angels on earth disguised as strangers we had yet to meet.

I remember the first time I was exposed to autism on anything more than a casual basis. I was the Director of Public Relations at Richmond International Raceway, one of the most popular NASCAR and IndyCar tracks in the country. Working there was the type of fun, high-profile sports job I dreamed about as a kid, and I worked with many amazing people, companies, and causes.

One of the NASCAR drivers I worked with to promote our events was from nearby Emporia, Virginia. Hermie Sadler has a daughter on the autism spectrum, and he called one day and asked track president Doug Fritz and me if we would be interested in organizing a benefit event for a nearby school for children with autism. Knowing the good work Hermie and Angie Sadler were doing, we were delighted to help. We organized a go-kart racing event with several NASCAR drivers and helped the Sadler's raise a nice amount of money for The Faison School for Autism in Richmond.

My exposure to the disorder began to grow as other autism organizations became involved with NASCAR on a larger scale. I had no idea that one day in the near future I would need to learn so much more about autism.

After our son was diagnosed, my learning curve was quickly accelerated thanks to many wonderful people. I emailed Hermie Sadler then spoke with Angie. They were incredibly supportive and helpful as two of those angels on earth. My brother and sister-in-law, Tom and Val, arranged for a meeting with Dr. David Sidener, the head of The Garden Academy, a school for children with autism here in New Jersey, where we now live.

It was a terrifying time. Our son was communicating in one or two words. When he was hungry, he would stand next to the refrigerator or pantry instead of telling us what he wanted. We were learning that the autism "spectrum" meant literally just that, a wide range or spectrum of intellect, agility, strength, communication, temperament, and ability to focus.

During our morning together, Dr. Sidener shared many great nuggets of information and wisdom with Donna and me, but there was one thing in particular that we took to heart and have never forgotten regarding our son's care: "You're in a race against time."

Studies show that early intervention is key to helping a child with a disability to succeed, especially one with an autism diagnosis. That intervention could mean many types of care, including speech therapy, occupational therapy, physical therapy, applied behavior analysis, and many other types of conventional and non-traditional methods of treatment. For our son, some of these types of therapies started around the time he was two, which was after the first neurology appointment but before the formal diagnosis at the next visit.

Watching these therapists help our son in our home or at an office was amazing and inspiring. We were not sure of the best ways to manage his stimming, hold his attention, redirect him when needed, or as crazy as it sounds, the most effective ways to interact with him. The weeks of therapy turned to months, the months grew to years, and our son's improvement and our ability as parents to help him have been nothing short of remarkable.

As we began to see the steady progress our son was making thanks to his hard work and the amazing professionals helping him, it occurred to me that it made sense to do something for the autism community. I contemplated starting an autism-related nonprofit foundation. There are so many great organizations doing incredible work in research and funding programs that I was not sure how I could make an impact.

One day it finally hit me. Education has played a huge role in my life. My mom was a remedial reading teacher for more than 30 years. My wife has taught at every level from elementary through college, and as an adjunct faculty member, I have had the pleasure of sharing my sports marketing and PR experience with students at several universities. But when the stakes were the highest and our son needed the expertise we were not properly equipped to provide, many amazing, highly-skilled professionals and therapists entered our lives to give our family guidance.

Our family is very grateful for the care and expertise we have received, but our experience also highlighted a serious math problem. More than 60,000 children are being diagnosed with autism each year. Our public school and public and private healthcare systems simply can't keep up with the demand for special education teachers, paraprofessionals, and therapists to work with individuals who have autism.

As a result, I started the Autism MVP Foundation in 2015. The organization is dedicated to increasing the number and quality of autism-focused educators and therapists. Over our first four years, we have begun to make a difference by starting a scholarship program for graduate students who are committed to a career that will improve educational, social, and daily life skill outcomes for individuals with autism. We also have partnered with Monmouth University in New Jersey, to underwrite the groundbreaking Autism Program Improvement Project. Through that program, two educators in Monmouth's School of Education work with public school districts to review their autism programs and observe their interaction with their autistic students. Then they take the collected data and feed it back to both the participating districts and their students pursuing a career in autism studies.

Along with my foundation work, my jobs working at the Gift of Life Donor program in Philadelphia, and later, in the community relations department at the Philadelphia 76ers gave me a chance to see up close the importance of and the intricacies of social impact-minded organizations.

My career path also led me to my co-author, Stan Phelps. After helping him collect more than 1,000 examples for his first book, *Purple Goldfish,* and providing editing assistance for that edition, I continued to follow his work, hoping that one day we could work together again.

I continued to follow Stan's work, and one of his books in particular caught my eye. *Red Goldfish* centered around the power of purpose and its growing importance in the workplace. It focused on how for-profit organizations were embracing putting purpose at the forefront of their enterprises to attract the best talent and win the hearts and minds of employees and customers.

My work with the Autism MVP Foundation reminded me that nonprofits are like any other type of business—they need a value proposition and a key differentiator in the marketplace to separate them from the competition in order to attract the best board members, employees, donors, and other supporters.

The competition is fierce in the nonprofit world, even when competing in different spaces. This book will explore the signature ways nonprofits reinforce their purpose and stand out in a crowded marketplace, whether it is an extra level of recognition for key donors, a special incentive designed to keep their best employees, or something simple like a luncheon to recognize volunteers or highest fundraisers. If you work at a nonprofit, we hope this book will help you deliver "a little extra" to your stakeholders.

PART I:

WHAT IS A RED GOLDFISH?

CHAPTER 1

THE EVOLUTION OF THE NONPROFIT

"To try and make the world in some way better than when you found it is to have a noble motive in life."

– Andrew Carnegie from *The Empire of Business*

Why are we here? This is perhaps the greatest question of all. It has been pondered since the earliest days of human existence. It is our search for meaning in this world. Each one of us is challenged to answer this question. Mark Twain once said that the two most important days in our lives are the day we are born and the day we found out why. As the number and type of nonprofits continue to proliferate, it is clear that the "why" question applies to businesses designed to "do good" in the world.

Taking a step back, why do nonprofits exist? What or who comes first? Where is the main focus? We believe there are five schools of thought that have evolved over the years.

The first school of thought we'll call the 1.0 version.

NONPROFIT 1.0 - BENEFICIARY-CENTERED

The 1.0 version in the evolution of a nonprofit was a beneficiary-first mindset. The sole purpose of an organization was to maximize efforts to benefit a cause.

The next evolution of a nonprofit places the focus squarely on donors first.

NONPROFIT 2.0 - DONOR-CENTERED

The 2.0 nonprofit version sees benefit as an end result, not the goal. Nonprofits should be dedicated to the business of getting and keeping donors. This focus places an importance on the overall donor experience and managing ongoing relationships. To paraphrase a quote by Walmart's founder, Sam Walton, "There is only one boss. The donor. And he or she can fire everybody in the company from the chairman on down, simply by giving his or her money somewhere else."

In this view, nonprofits should stop defining themselves by their benefit. Instead they should reorient themselves toward donor needs. In his best-known *Harvard Business Review* article, "Marketing Myopia," Theodore Levitt made the case for organizations to shift their focus. He used the railroad industry to illustrate the point.

> The railroads did not stop growing because the need for passenger and freight transportation declined. That grew. The railroads are in trouble today not because that need was filled by others (cars, trucks, airplanes, and even telephones) but because it was *not* filled by the railroads themselves. They let others take customers away from them because they assumed themselves to be in the railroad business rather than in the transportation business. The reason they defined their industry incorrectly was that they were railroad oriented instead of transportation oriented; they were product oriented instead of customer oriented.[1]

Peter Drucker made a similar argument about focus in his classic book, *Management,* when he wrote, "There is only one valid definition of business purpose: to create a customer [donor] . . . . It is the customer [donor] who determines what a business [nonprofit] is. It is the customer [donor] alone whose willingness to pay for a good or for a service converts economic resources into wealth, things into goods, the customer [donor] is the foundation of a business [nonprofit] and keeps it in existence."

The next version of a nonprofit puts volunteers at the forefront.

---

1. https://hbr.org/2006/10/what-business-are-you-in-classic-advice-from-theodore-levitt

NONPROFIT 3.0 - VOLUNTEER FIRST

Some nonprofits exist to ensure that volunteers are aware of opportunities in their respective communities, thus making a volunteer-focused model stronger and more of a focus. Points of Light designs "products and services that make it easier for volunteers to find opportunities to serve, for nonprofits to collaborate and share resources, and to ensure dedicated volunteers are recognized for their commitment to doing good."[2]

The next version of a nonprofit places staff at the forefront.

NONPROFIT 4.0 - STAFF FIRST

The 4.0 version of nonprofit places employees first. It is rooted in understanding where value is created in an organization. It's is created in the last two feet of a transaction, the space between the employee and the customer. Former HCL Technologies CEO Vineet Nayar calls these 24 inches the *"value zone."* Nayar made employees the priority at HCL, putting employees first, customers second, management third, and shareholders last. He believed front-line employees were the true custodians of the brand and drivers of customer loyalty. Nayar wanted to shift the focus from the "WHAT" of what HCL offered to the "HOW" of delivering value.

A focus on staff first is based on the idea that culture trumps strategy in an organization. The experience of your employees becomes paramount as it dictates your overall culture. "I came to see in my time at IBM that 'culture' isn't just one aspect of the game–it is the game," says Lou Gerstner, former IBM CEO and author of *Who Says Elephants Can't Dance.*

2. https://www.pointsoflight.org/products-and-services/

In today's workplace, up to 70 percent of workers are either not engaged or are actively disengaged. To be successful, you need staff who are engaged to create a strong customer experience. According to Ted Coiné, author of *Five Star Customer Service,* "You can't create happy enthused customers without happy engaged employees." The same holds true in the nonprofit world.

The next evolution of a nonprofit places purpose and the greater good as the critical first piece of the puzzle.

NONPROFIT 5.0 – PURPOSE AND GREATER GOOD FIRST

The 5.0 version of a nonprofit places mission/purpose and the greater good first. Nonprofits that have a strong, defined purpose find that it drives staff engagement, connects with volunteers, and fuels donations. According to Deloitte Global CEO Punit Renjen, "Exceptional firms have always been good at aligning their purpose with their execution, and as a result have enjoyed category leadership."

Purpose relates to your "Why" as a nonprofit. To quote Simon Sinek, "People don't buy what you do or how you do it, they buy why you do it." It should permeate everything you do. "Every decision should be looked at in terms of purpose. Some decisions may be purpose neutral. But purpose is certainly not just a marketing issue or positioning of your brand image. Purpose should impact every aspect," says Raj Sisodia, author of *Conscious Capitalism* and FW Olin Distinguished Professor of Global Business at Babson College.

Embracing purpose can become a driver of staff engagement. Daniel Pink touched on the importance of purpose in his book *Drive.* Pink said there are three things that motivate people: autonomy, mastery, and purpose. He believes that purpose is perhaps the greatest of the three, because a strong purpose allows you to overcome obstacles and persevere toward a goal.

In many respects, our world is changing for the better as the younger generations in the marketplace embrace purpose as a key driver in the companies they seek to work for or even the ones they want to start. In fact, 1 in 10 "Gen Zers" wants to start their own charity.[3]

As a result—and knowing that 70 percent of high schoolers want to volunteer at a charity to gain work experience[4]—there may not be a better time to start and run a nonprofit, especially in the U.S. According to the National Center for Charitable Statistics, there are more than 1.5 million nonprofit organizations in the U.S. that employ 11.5 million people.[5] These organizations are public charities, private foundations, and other types of nonprofits such as chambers of commerce and civic leagues. Collectively, these groups are known as NGOs or Non-governmental organizations, which according to grantspace.org is a term originally coined by the United Nations in 1945. Globally, there are an estimated 10 million NGOs, and if NGOs were a country, that country would have the fifth largest population in the world.[6]

NEW WAY FORWARD

The old view of a nonprofit was a beneficiary-first mindset. You put beneficiaries first, donors second, volunteers third, staff fourth, and purpose last in terms of focus.

---

3. http://millennialbranding.com/2014/high-school-careers-study/
4. https://trust.guidestar.org/nonprofits-and-generation-z
5. https://grantspace.org/resources/knowledge-base/number-of-nonprofits-in-the-u-s/
6. http://ccss.jhu.edu/

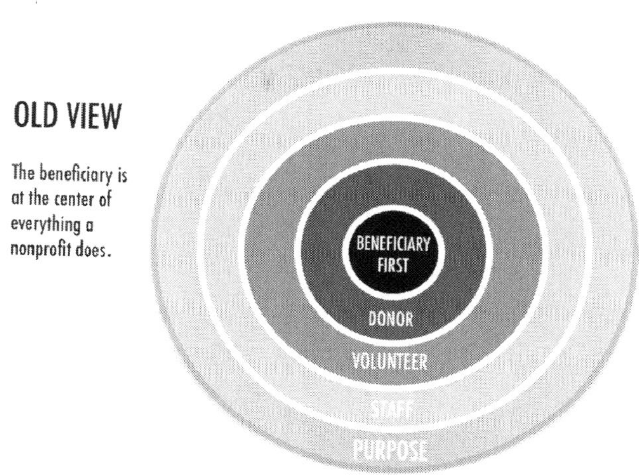

An emerging view of a nonprofit going forward goes beyond a beneficiary-first mindset. It is the exact opposite of the traditional approach. You put purpose at the center of everything the nonprofit does. Then staff comes second, volunteers third, and the donors fourth. Taking care of those four, the beneficiary receives the result as opposed to being the sole aim.

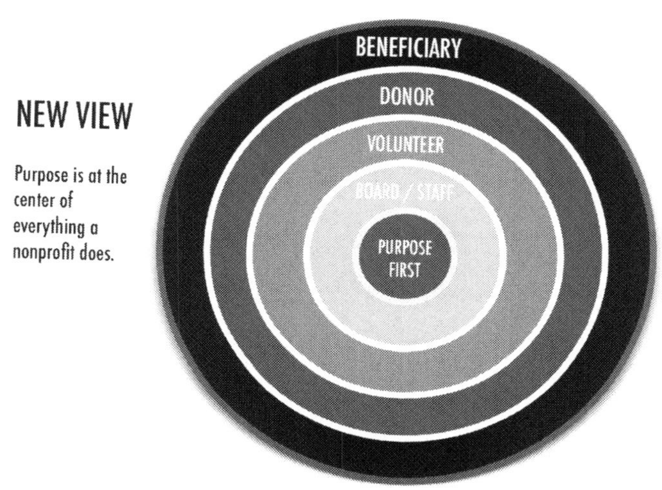

CHAPTER 2

THE BLURRING OF LINES

"Well run, values-centered businesses can contribute to humankind in more tangible ways than any other organization in society."

– Bill George, Former CEO Medtronic

Purpose is changing the way we work and do business for the foreseeable future. It is our belief that during the next decade there will no longer be a large distinction between for-profit companies and nonprofit organizations. The evolution of corporate social responsibility, benefit corporations, new nonprofit models, and the conscious capitalism movement have forever blurred the line of how we look at organizations. Nonprofits no longer are alone in pursuing the greater good. Business is changing.

The traditional view of business was binary. A distinction between organizations was made based on corporate filing status. You were either a for-profit or a nonprofit organization.

Today the lines are not so clear, yet it is important to analyze the many different types of for-profit organizations and nonprofits. The emergence of social media has increased transparency in business. It has shined a light on the intentions of organizations. Purpose is now becoming a differentiator in business. Beyond products and features, consumers now want to know the "why" behind an organization.

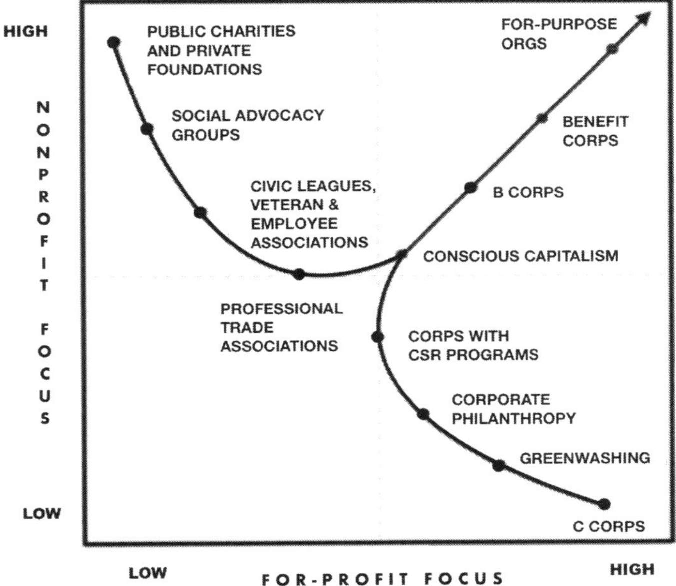

Let's look at the variations among the different types of for-profit and nonprofit organizations and the accompanying methods they often use to conduct their business, starting with nonprofits.

1. **Public Charities.** These are the largest type of nonprofits in the United States with nearly one million organizations. They do not seek profit. In the U.S, these organizations must be approved by the Internal Revenue Service to be tax-exempt under the terms of section 501(c)(3) of the Internal Revenue Code. Examples include food banks, amateur sports associations, animal welfare organizations, art museums, and organizations seeking a cure or raising awareness around a disease or disorder. The code dictates that tax-exemptions can apply to entities that are organized and operated exclusively for religious, charitable, scientific, literary, or educational purposes, or for testing for public safety, or to foster national or international amateur sports competition, or for the prevention of cruelty to children or animals.

2. **Private Foundations.** Generally, these 501(c)(3) organizations exist to support other nonprofits. There are more than 100,000 of these types of organizations in the United States. The key difference between private foundations and public charities is that private foundations are required to give a certain amount of their income annually. Prominent examples include the Bill and Melinda Gates Foundation, the Walton Family Foundation, and the Ford Foundation.

3. **Social Advocacy Groups.** Social advocacy groups fall under the 501(c)(4) umbrella and are generally organized to promote a social or political cause. These organizations are not allowed to accept tax deductible individual donations and typically do not receive grants. Instead, they are permitted to participate in nearly unlimited lobbying activities to

further their cause.[7] Although smaller organizations that are not political or social in nature can still fall under the 501(c)(4) umbrella, prominent examples are Greenpeace, the ACLU, and the NRA.

4. **Professional Trade Associations.** These organizations fall under the 501(c)(6) designation and exist to advance the business purpose of its members. Examples include PRSA (Public Relations Society of America), NKBA (National Kitchen and Bath Association), and the ANA (Association of National Advertisers). Generally, these organizations are funded by membership dues and are permitted to engage in lobbying efforts on behalf of its constituents.

5. **Nonprofit with a Revenue Model.** Some nonprofits blend social mission and commercial enterprise. As government funding sources have dried up and competition for foundation grants has gotten more intense, nonprofits are starting to embrace earned revenue opportunities. Colleges and universities fall into this category even though they are public charities. These organizations generally rely on various, consistent forms of revenue streams such as state government funding and tuition fees.

Now, let's look at for-profits

1. **Greenwashing.** Whitewashing is a coordinated attempt to hide unpleasant facts, typically in a political context. Greenwashing is the same premise but in an environmental context in business. Greenwashing is when a company or organization spends more time and money claiming to be "green" through advertising and marketing than

7. https://www.foundationsource.com/learn-about-foundations/what-is-a-private-foundation/

actually implementing business practices that minimize environmental impact.[8]

2. **Corporate Philanthropy.** Corporate philanthropy is the act of a corporation or business promoting the welfare of others, generally via charitable donations of funds or time. Charity and philanthropy are often used interchangeably, however, this should not be the case. According to *Philanthropy in America: A History,* the difference between the two is that "charity relieves the pains of social problems, whereas philanthropy attempts to solve these problems at their root." Corporate philanthropy is often focused on treating the issues that nonprofit organizations exist to serve. Corporate philanthropy can come through a variety of channels—monetary donations or gifts of time and talent (in-kind donations). Commonly, these may be matching gifts, volunteer grants, and any other type of product or service donation that is non-monetary.

3. **Corporate Capitalism.** Corporate Social Responsibility (CSR) is a concept whereby companies integrate social and environmental concerns in their business operations and in their interaction with their stakeholders on a voluntary basis. It happens when organizations go beyond minimum legal requirements and obligations to address societal needs. CSR is a form of corporate self-regulation integrated into a business model. The aim is to increase long-term profits and shareholder trust through positive public relations and high ethical standards to reduce business and legal risk by taking responsibility for corporate actions. CSR strategies encourage the company to make a positive impact on the environment and stakeholders including consumers, employees, investors, communities, and others.[9]

8. http://greenwashingindex.com/about-greenwashing/
9. http://digitalcommons.liberty.edu/cgi/viewcontent.cgi?article=1229&context=honors

4. **Conscious Capitalism.** Conscious Capitalism is a term created by John Mackey and Raj Sisodia. It is a global movement to elevate humanity and awaken the heroic spirit of business. The idea is based on the notion that capitalism can be a force both for economic and social good. There are four components to Conscious Capitalism. 1. **Higher Purpose** - Conscious Businesses focus on their purpose beyond profit. 2. **Stakeholder Integration** - Conscious Businesses focus on their whole business ecosystem, creating and optimizing value for all of their stakeholders. Conscious Business is a win-win-win proposition as it includes a healthy return to shareholders. 3. **Conscious Leadership** - Conscious Leaders focus on "we" rather than "me." They inspire, foster transformation, and bring out the best in those around them. They recognize the integral role of culture and purposefully cultivate a Conscious Culture of trust and care. 4. **Conscious Culture** - Culture is the embodied values, principles, and practices underlying the social fabric of a business. This culture permeates the company's actions and connects the stakeholders to each other and to the company's purpose, people, and processes.[10]

5. **B Corp Certification.** B Corp certification is a third-party certification by B Lab. The certification is based on the following key items: measurable social performance, accountability, transparency, and measurable environmental performance. The B Corp designation was established in Wayne, Pennsylvania by founders Jay Coen Gilbert, Bart Houlahan, and Andrew Kassoy. They introduced the certified B Corp standard in 2007. The B Corp is a voluntary certification and can be dropped at any time. There are fees involved with certification as well as future audits to ensure compliance with all of the standards.

10. https://hbr.org/2013/04/companies-that-practice-conscious-capitalism-perform\

6. **Benefit Corporation**. A benefit corporation is a true legal entity classification for a for-profit business. Social entrepreneurs can choose this classification to mirror their desires for fiduciary and environmental responsibility. Benefit corporations must commit to the following: "Making a material positive impact on society and the environment." The legal documents utilized in creating this type of a corporation are required to consider the consequences of all key actions as they affect stakeholders, not just shareholders. All existing corporate laws still pertain and leadership must still report on the corporation's efforts via current third-party standards. More than 30 U.S. states have enacted laws to recognize a benefit corporation.

It is important for nonprofits to understand how for-profit businesses are leveraging purpose to drive both customer and employee engagement. The bar has been raised. The need to differentiate is more important than ever and can open new doors to innovation.

CHAPTER 3

PURPOSE IS THE NEW BLACK

"Corporate purpose is at the confluence of strategy and values. It expresses the company's fundamental—the raison d'être or overriding reason for existing. It is the end to which the strategy is directed."

– Richard Ellsworth

Purpose is becoming the new black. Beyond just mission, purpose is emerging as a guiding light that can help organizations navigate and thrive in the twenty-first century. According to the EY Beacon Institute Pursuit of Purpose Study, "Purpose—an aspirational reason for being that is grounded in humanity—is at the core of how many companies are responding to the business and societal challenges of today."

What can happen if you put purpose at the core of your nonprofit to drive differentiation and engagement? Here are 10 benefits from the EY Purpose Study:[11]

1. Purpose instills strategic clarity.
2. Purpose guides both short-term decisions and long-term strategy at every level of an organization, encouraging leaders to think about systems holistically.
3. Purpose guides choices about what not to do as well as what to do.
4. Purpose channels innovation.
5. Purpose is a force for and a response to transformation.
6. Purpose motivates people through meaning, not fear. It clarifies the long-term outcome so people understand the need for change rather than feeling it is imposed upon them.
7. Purpose is also a response to societal pressures on business to transform, to address global challenges, and to take a longer-term, more comprehensive approach to growth and value.

11. http://www.ey.com/Publication/vwLUAssets/EY-pursuit-of-purpose-exec-sum/$FILE/EY-pursuit-of-purpose-exec-sum.pdf

8. Purpose taps a universal need to contribute, to feel part of society.

9. Purpose recognizes differences and diversity. Purpose builds bridges.

10. Purpose helps individuals/teams to work across silos to pursue a single, compelling aim.

WIN-WIN-WIN

Nonprofits with a strong, defined purpose benefit from a win-win-win scenario. They are winning on three levels:

Win #1: Staff - Purpose helps attract the best talent, keeps them engaged, and retains them. It is important to employees as it helps define the values of an organization. According to PriceWaterhouseCoopers. "6 out of 7 employees would consider leaving an employer whose values no longer met their expectations."[12]

Win #2: Donors - Purpose becomes a differentiator that drives acquisition and retention. It also helps the organization stay competitive. It provides a reason for their donors to engage. Purpose is important to donors and other stakeholders as it showcases the values of an organization. According to Brand Fuel, "All things being equal, 6 out of 7 people will choose to do business with organizations whose values mesh with their own."

Win #3: Volunteers - Purpose is a main driver of why individuals volunteer for nonprofits, and a personal connection often fuels that engagement. But even if an individual's motivation also includes career development, networking opportunities, or building

12. https://www.pwc.com/m1/en/services/consulting/documents/millennials-at-work.pdf

self-esteem or confidence, purpose is the underlying unifier that brings people together to give their time to a cause they care about.

BRINGING PURPOSE TO LIFE

According to Gallup, when it comes to communicating an organization's purpose to your employees, donors, and staff, words don't matter nearly as much as actions do. Nonprofits need to find ways to bring purpose to life to drive engagement. Creating little things that can make a big difference for both staff, volunteers, and donors is one way to bring purpose to life. "It's easy to state a purpose and state a set of values. It's much harder to enact them in the organization because it requires you to continually search for consistency across many disciplines and many activities," says Michael Beer. We call the little things that can be done to drive engagement and bring purpose to life a Red Goldfish. In the next two chapters, we will explain the meaning behind this term, including why red and why a goldfish.

CHAPTER 4

WHY A GOLDFISH?

"Big doors swing on little hinges"

- W. Clement Stone

The origin of the goldfish in *Red Goldfish* dates back to 2009 when the Purple Goldfish crowdsourcing project began. It has become the signature element of the book series. A goldfish represents something small, but despite its size, something with the ability to make a big difference.

Part of the inspiration for the goldfish came from Kimpton Hotels. In 2001, the boutique hotel chain's Hotel Monaco began offering travelers a temporary travel companion for the duration of their stay. Perhaps the guests were traveling on business and getting a little lonely. Or maybe they were with family and missing the family pet. Whatever the case, Kimpton came to the rescue. Kimpton guests can temporarily adopt a goldfish for their stay. They call the program Guppy Love. The goldfish has now become a signature element of the Kimpton experience with the program attracting national attention.

"The Guppy Love program is a fun extension of our pet-friendly nature as well as our emphasis on indulging the senses to heighten the travel experience," says Steve Pinetti, Senior Vice President of Sales & Marketing for Kimpton Hotels and Restaurants. "Everything about Hotel Monaco appeals directly to the senses, and 'Guppy Love' offers one more unique way to relax, indulge and promote health of mind, body and spirit in our home-away-from-home atmosphere."

Guppy Love inspired the start of the Purple Goldfish Project. Three years later in 2012, the book *Purple Goldfish* was published. This Amazon Bestseller was followed by *Green Goldfish* in 2013 and *Golden Goldfish* in 2014. *Blue Goldfish* became the fourth color in the series in 2016. The original Red Goldfish was published in 2017. Since then, *Pink Goldfish* and *Yellow Goldfish* came in 2018. *Gray Goldfish* followed in 2019.

The size of a goldfish is relevant to the series. The overarching concept is the idea that little things can make the biggest difference. The growth of a goldfish became a metaphor for business. The average common goldfish is between three and four inches in length (10 cm), yet the largest in the world is almost six times that size. Imagine walking down the street and bumping into someone 30 feet tall (9 meters). How can there be such a disparity between a regular goldfish and their monster-size cousins? It turns out that the growth of the goldfish is determined by five distinct factors. The growth of a business is similar to that of a goldfish. Like goldfish, not all businesses will grow equally.

The growth of a goldfish and the growth of a business are affected by the following five factors:

#1. Size of the Bowl or Pond = The Market

> GROWTH FACTOR: The size of the bowl or pond
>
> RULE OF THUMB: Direct correlation. The larger the bowl or pond, the larger the goldfish can grow. The smaller the market, the smaller the business growth opportunity.

#2. Number of Other Goldfish in the Pond = Competition

> GROWTH FACTOR: The number of goldfish in the same bowl or pond
>
> RULE OF THUMB: Inverse correlation. The more goldfish, the less growth. The less competition, the more business growth opportunity.

#3. Nutrients and Cloudiness of the Water = The Economy

> GROWTH FACTOR: The cloudiness of the water and the level of nutrients in the water

RULE OF THUMB: Direct correlation. The more nutrients and better clarity, the larger the growth. The less access to capital or reduced consumer confidence, the more difficult it is for a business to grow.

Sidebar: Fact

A malnourished goldfish in a crowded, cloudy environment may only grow to two inches (five centimeters).

#4. Its first 120 days of life = Startup Phase or Product Launch

GROWTH FACTOR: The nourishment and treatment they receive as a baby goldfish

RULE OF THUMB: Direct correlation. The lower the quality of the food, water, and treatment, the more the goldfish will be stunted for future growth. The stronger the leadership and capital as a start-up, the better the business growth.

Fact - A baby goldfish is called a fry. They are tiny when they are born, literally a "small fry."

#5. Its Genetic Makeup = Differentiation

GROWTH FACTOR: The genetic makeup of the goldfish

RULE OF THUMB: Direct correlation. The weaker the genes or the less differentiated, the less the goldfish can grow. The more differentiated the product or service from the competition, the better the chance for business growth.

Fact - The longest goldfish according to *Guinness World Records* is from the Netherlands at a lengthy

18.7 inches (50 cm).[13] To put that in perspective, that's the size of the average domesticated cat.

Which of the five factors can you control?

Let's assume you have an existing product or service and have been in business for more than four months. Do you have any control over the market, your competition, or the economy? NO, NO, and NO. The only thing you have control over is your business's genetic makeup or how you differentiate your product or service.

It is our belief that purpose is becoming the ultimate differentiator. How are you leveraging purpose in your nonprofit? In goldfish terms, how are you standing out in a sea of sameness?

13. https://www.guinnessworldrecords.com/world-records/longest-goldfish?fb_comment_id=620394178066310_736851779753882

CHAPTER 5

WHY RED?

"We picked up one excellent word—a word
worth traveling to New Orleans to get;
a nice limber, expressive, handy word—lagniappe"

- Mark Twain

Red is the fifth color in the Goldfish series of books. The initial color trilogy was an ode to an iconic American city and its most famous event. That city is New Orleans. Purple, green, and gold are the three official colors of Mardi Gras. It is a reference to New Orleans because there is one word from New Orleans that exemplifies the concept of doing the little something extra. That word is lagniappe. Pronounced *lan-yap,* it is a creole word meaning an "added gift" or "to give more." The practice originated in Louisiana in the 1840s whereby a merchant would give a customer a little something extra at the time of purchase. It is a signature personal touch by the business that creates goodwill and promotes word of mouth.

Mark Twain was smitten with the word. He wrote about lagniappe in the book *Life on the Mississippi*:[14]

> We picked up one excellent word–a word worth traveling to New Orleans to get; a nice limber, expressive, handy word–"lagniappe." They pronounce it lanny-yap. It is Spanish–so they said. We discovered it at the head of a column of odds and ends in the [Times] Picayune [newspaper] the first day; heard twenty people use it the second; inquired what it meant the third; adopted it and got facility in swinging it the fourth. It has a restricted meaning, but I think the people spread it out a little when they choose. It is the equivalent of the thirteenth roll in a baker's dozen. It is something thrown in, gratis, for good measure. The custom originated in the Spanish quarter of the city.

In the trilogy, *Purple Goldfish* focused on the little things you could do to improve the customer experience, *Green Goldfish* examined how to drive engagement to improve the employee experience, and

14. https://books.google.com/books/about/Life_on_the_Mississippi.html?id=t8A280enLZIC&printsec=frontcover&source=kp_read_button#v=onepage&q&f=false

the third book, *Golden Goldfish,* uncovered the importance of taking care of your best customers/employees.

The fourth book, *Blue Goldfish,* revealed how to leverage technology, data, and analytics to improve the customer and employee experience. Blue was a reference to a tenth century Danish king named Harald Gormsson. Gormsson united Scandinavia and converted the Danes to Christianity. His nickname was Bluetooth, a reference to a dead tooth that had turned blue. In the 1990s, Bluetooth became the name for the wireless area networking standard we use today. Blue highlights convergence, just as Bluetooth was the result of a consortium and King Harald united Scandinavia. Our convergence is big data and little data coming together to deliver high-level personalized experiences.

WHY RED?

Red is the color of blood. Historically it is associated with sacrifice and courage. In the US and Europe, red also represents passion, whereas in Asia, it symbolizes happiness and good fortune. We, however, went farther afield for our source. Our inspiration for the red in the original *Red Goldfish* book comes from Africa.

(RED) was created by Bono and Bobby Shriver.[15] Launched at the World Economic Forum in 2006, its purpose was to engage the private sector and its marketing prowess in order to raise funds for the fight against AIDS in Africa. On the back of a napkin, they outlined their idea for a unique union of brands and consumers. The plan had three goals:

1. Provide consumers with a choice that made giving effortless

2. Generate profits and a sense of purpose for partner companies

15. htttp://www.wolffolins.com/work/37/red

3. Create a source of sustainable income for the Global Fund to fund the fight against AIDS

(RED) was a continuation of work for Africa by U2's lead singer. In 2002, Bono co-founded DATA (Debt, AIDS, Trade, Africa), a platform to raise public awareness of the issues in its name and influence government policy on Africa. In 2004, DATA helped to create ONE: The Campaign to Make Poverty History. ONE is dedicated to fighting extreme poverty and preventable disease. In early 2008, DATA and ONE combined operations under the ONE organization.

Prior to the launch of (RED), businesses had contributed just $5 million to the Global Fund in four years. In a decade since its inception, the private sector, through (RED), has contributed more than $400 million. One hundred percent of the funds are invested in HIV/AIDS programs in Africa with a focus on countries with high prevalence of mother-to-child transmission of HIV.

Global brands such as Apple, Nike, Dell, American Express, and The Gap came on board. The appeal of (RED) was clear: it allowed them to tap into a purpose beyond their own profit. Partner brands created special (RED) versions of products and a portion of the profits from the sales go to the Global Fund to fight malaria, tuberculosis, and AIDS.

(RED) helped reinforce the simple idea that doing good is good business for both customers and employees. American Express saw an immediate lift in brand perception with younger customers, while GAP saw a major improvement in employee engagement as well as the quality of incoming recruits. Their INSPI(RED) T-shirt became the biggest seller in their history.

Red represents the simple idea that organizations can be a force for good in the world. Our inspiration for red in the *Red Goldfish*

Nonprofit Edition is Clarissa Harlowe Barton. Clarissa, known as Clara, was working in the US Patent Office when the Civil War began. Like many women, she helped collect bandages and other much-needed supplies for the Union troops. Barton soon realized that she could best support the troops by going in person to the battlefields. Known as the "Angel of the Battlefield," she nursed, comforted, and cooked for the wounded in the field.

When the war end, Barton traveled to Europe. There, she became aware of the Geneva, Switzerland-based Red Cross. According to the American Red Cross,[16] upon her return home, Barton was determined that the United States should participate in the global Red Cross network. Working with influential friends and contacts such as Frederick Douglass, she founded the American Red Cross in 1881. Barton served as president of the organization until 1904, when she resigned at age 83.

Red is a prominent color for nonprofits whether it is the American Red Cross, the Salvation Army, Save the Children, St. Jude Children's Hospital, or the YMCA.

Now let's look at the different ways to drive engagement for donors, volunteers, board members, and staff. Let's go . . .

16. https://www.redcross.org/about-us/who-we-are/history/clara-barton.html

PART II:

TYPES OF ENGAGEMENT

CHAPTER 6

VOLUNTEER ENGAGEMENT

"Service to others is the rent you pay for your room here on earth."

- Muhammad Ali

According to the most recent volunteering statistics available from the United States Department of Labor, nearly 63 million Americans representing 24.9 percent of the population volunteered in 2015. That figure represents an amazing 7.8 billion hours of service[17] but marks a decline from when volunteerism was at is peak between 2003 and 2005 and 28.9 percent of Americans volunteered.[18]

But while overall volunteering numbers have declined, it is important to note that the ways we can volunteer have changed drastically since that peak period of the early years of the previous decade. Volunteers can now assist virtually and be paired quickly with a cause they care about in their community via any number of volunteer-matching websites to share their time, treasure, and talents.

The relationship between an organization and its volunteers is symbiotic. Volunteers are nearly twice as likely (nearly 80 percent vs. 40 percent) to give to charity as non-volunteers, and volunteers who are out of work have a 27 percent higher chance of finding a job than those who do not volunteer. In addition, volunteers without a high school diploma have a 51 percent higher chance of finding work, and 55 percent of volunteers in rural areas have a better chance of finding work than non-volunteers.[19]

It is also important to be cognizant of marketplace conditions and how they can affect volunteer numbers and retention rates. For example, a study showed that people in larger metropolitan areas with longer commute times will volunteer less, and a change of just three minutes in commuting time can decrease volunteering by 2.3 percent.[20] It is also interesting to note that the states listed

17. https://www.bls.gov/news.release/volun.nr0.htm
18. https://www.nationalservice.gov/vcla/national
19. https://www.nationalservice.gov/vcla/research
20. https://www.nationalservice.gov/vcla/research

below have the highest success rate in retaining their volunteers. Perhaps with less recreational options and few large metropolitan areas, nonprofits in these sparsely-populated states can have better retention rates:

Vermont

Utah

North Dakota

South Dakota

Idaho[5]

Regardless, retaining volunteers can be difficult in this day and age. We have more distractions, and there are more organizations to volunteer for than ever before—the 1.5 million nonprofits in the US roughly average just shy of 3,000 per state since 2005.[21]

Retention strategies are key and many of them are simple, even for the nonprofit foundations that are run entirely by volunteers themselves. Here are a few ways to boost retention rates during each aspect of the volunteering cycle (pre-event, during the event, post-event):

- Ask via an email, phone call, or meeting what a volunteer wants to get out of the experience. This is an important aspect of your on-boarding process. For example, perhaps a high school student needs a letter to verify a service hour requirement or an executive out of work wants to expand his network. Find out how they heard about your organization, what motivated them to get involved, what their special skills are, and how they prefer to be contacted (email, phone, text).

21. https://www.nationalservice.gov/vcla/state-rankings-volunteer-retention-rate

- Track your volunteers' efforts by keeping their information in your database, even if they have yet to make a charitable contribution.

- Be organized on site! This is critical. Nobody likes to spend their time if things aren't organized for them and their assignments aren't clear. Along the same lines, ensure that their efforts match with their skill set and interests so you can maximize their involvement.

- This sounds basic, but communicate with them consistently, not only to thank them for their efforts but to emphasize how their time made an event possible or helped raise even more money. That communication should also incorporate information about future volunteering opportunities with the organization.

What are some specific tactics that organizations use to attract and retain volunteers? Some of the best retention ideas are simple, don't cost much or any money, and can go a long way toward keeping your volunteers engaged, productive, and happy to share their experience with other potential volunteers.

- Create an award

- Highlight volunteer efforts in a newsletter

- Leverage a special occasion to host recognition events, such as National Volunteer Week

- Mix up your communication—do more than emails—texting and face-to-face times are good

- Study the characteristics of highest-contributing volunteers and apply them to others you seek

- Create a unique program
- Create a volunteer engagement scale

All of these elements are critical to a nonprofit's overall health and future if for no other reasons than the following:[22]

- Volunteers donate ten times more than non-volunteers—$2,593 per year vs. $230 per year.
- 67 percent of volunteers donate to the same charities where they volunteer.

Next, we will explore some of the best examples of engaging donors.

22. https://nccs.urban.org/publication/nonprofit-sector-brief-2018#highlights

CHAPTER 7

DONOR ENGAGEMENT

"As nonprofits continue to compete for the same donors and/or membership opportunities, individual giving programs will continue to evolve as fundraisers will find new and creative ways to engage donors. From increased social media giving to strategic influencer marketing campaigns, individuals will be a priority for organizational support."

— Lindrea Reynolds

When it comes to donor engagement and understanding what is important to making initial and repeat gifts, three key factors emerge: creative communication, leveraging technology, and providing incentives.

This is important because giving to a nonprofit—and choosing one that fits with an individual's interests and values—has never been easier. That is further reflected by the growth of nonprofit giving in the United States. In 2018, overall giving grew 4.1 percent, marking the sixth consecutive year of growth, while online giving grew 12.1 percent.[23]

The downside to this is that the philanthropic marketplace is crowded and the media landscape is fragmented, so it is more important than ever to creatively communicate with donors to maximize giving opportunities.

Many things can keep nonprofit board members and staff up at night, but this graphic represents what an annual decrease of just 20 percent of donors can mean, assuming an initial 1,000 contributors. For some, this is the difference between thriving and starting new initiatives, keeping the status quo, or even going out of business.

DONOR ATTRITION OVER A FIVE YEAR PERIOD

NUMBER OF DONORS	ATTRITION RATE	DONORS REMAINING AFTER 1 YEAR	DONORS REMAINING AFTER 2 YEARS	DONORS REMAINING AFTER 3 YEARS	DONORS REMAINING AFTER 4 YEARS	DONORS REMAINING AFTER 5 YEARS
1,000	20%	800	640	512	410	328
1,000	40%	600	360	216	130	78
1,000	60%	400	160	64	26	10

23. https://www.slideshare.net/bloomerang/everything-you-need-to-know-about-increasing-donor-and-board-member-engagement?qid=77a68be8-d83d-4481-b4b3-a8cfe2289c9e&v=&b=&from_search=12

What is most important in attracting and retaining donors? The public's trust in an organization is rated as the number one factor to influence the decision to engage (donate time and money).[24]

COMMUNICATING EFFECTIVELY

Once trust is established, it is up to a nonprofit to communicate creatively, harness the power of technology, and leverage data, all of which can be accomplished by using a strong Customer Relationship Management (CRM) platform. This is—or should be—the norm these days since the advantages are numerous.

For example, donor lists can be segmented in the following ways:[25]

1. Preferred communication channels
2. Frequency of communication
3. Affinities for certain programs
4. Generational demographics
5. Preferred giving channels
6. Annual gift levels

Once a donation is received, it is critical to follow up immediately. Consider how time-sensitive follow-up tactics can make an impact:

- First-time donors who get a personal thank you within 48 hours are four times more likely to give a second gift (Tom Ahern)[26]

24. https://www.slideshare.net/charitydynamics/participant-support-webinar?qid=d34d8796-4502-4157-95b3-107e8c5dce85&v=&b=&from_search=57
25. www.doublethedonation.com
26. https://bloomerang.co/blog/5-things-that-break-my-fundraising-heart/

- A three-minute thank-you call will boost first-year retention by 30 percent. (Roger Craver / The Agitator)[27]

- A thank-you call from a board member to a newly acquired donor within 24 hours of receiving a gift will increase their next gift by 39 percent.[28]

Overall, if a donor is guided properly, he or she is more likely to continue to give.

- 93 percent of individual donors would "definitely or probably" give again the next time they were asked if a charity thanked them promptly, in a personal way, and followed up later with a meaningful report on the program they had funded.

- 64 percent would give a larger gift.

- 74 percent would continue to give indefinitely.

- In addition, 46 percent of donors stop giving to a charity for reasons related to lack of meaningful information.[29]

Further, it is essential to have an impactful confirmation page once an online donation is received. Here are five critical steps.[30] Communicate that the donation was processed

1. Thank the donor and communicate the impact

2. Preview future communications

3. Give the donor something to do next

4. Keep them on the website to convert again!

27. https://nonprofitstorytellingconference.com/wp-content/uploads/2016/11/npsc16-segmentation-ss.pdf
28. https://trust.guidestar.org/blog/how-to-increase-donations-by-39
29. Burk, Penelope. Donor-Centered Fundraising. 2003
30. https://bloomerang.co/blog/21-ideas-for-your-nonprofits-donation-confirmation-page

An increasingly popular method that many nonprofits are using is video in their thank-you efforts to donors. Consider the following: [31]

- Including video in an email increases click-through rates by 200-300 percent
- 54 percent of people want to see videos from brands they support
- The average person retains 95 percent of what they watch in a video, compared to just 10 percent of a text message

When making thank-you videos, be mindful of the donor-first language:

- "We could not do this work without you."
- "Thank you for your partnership."
- "Thank you for your investment."
- "We are building something big together."
- "The work isn't done yet, but we have accomplished a lot."[32]

Leveraging these tactics to increase repeat gifts can make a substantial difference to a nonprofit's bottom-line, and data from donorCentrics reinforces this statistic: If a nonprofit is able to get a donor to make a sustaining gift, the benefits rise exponentially as sustaining contributions are worth up to four times more than those from traditional donors over the life of their giving. Twelve sustaining gifts in the typical range of $10–$25 each month is worth

31. https://medium.com/@juliacsocial/how-to-show-impact-in-your-nonprofit-donor-thank-you-video-7bb9422a4dd6
32. https://medium.com/@juliacsocial/how-to-show-impact-in-your-nonprofit-donor-thank-you-video-7bb9422a4dd6

more annual revenue than the majority of single-gift donors will contribute in the same period.

It is also critical to demonstrate the impact an organization is making in its communication to donors:

For example:[33]

1. How do we define our impact?
2. How do we know if we are making an impact?
3. How do we communicate our impact to others?
4. How do we evaluate our impact?
5. How can we increase our impact?

Examining the two distinct examples of communication below leads to an obvious conclusion of the better approach.

Example #1: Generic Giving Levels – How much would you like to donate?

$5

$10

$50

$100

$250

33. https://www.slideshare.net/blackbaud/back-to-basics-how-to-acquire-retain-and-upgrade-your-donors

Example #2: Productized Giving. How would you like to make an impact?

$5 Plant a tree

$10 One meal for a Senior

$350 One day of camp for cancer patient

$1,000 Keep a youth off the street

$2,500 Keep a student enrolled in college

Although a gift of $2,500 may not be the norm for many nonprofits, it is important to keep in mind the concept of lagniappe when engaging higher-end donors:

Although this is subjective, *Money* says the "the coolest rewards begin at the $1,000 level."[34]

For example, the common threads at attraction-based nonprofits include special access to private collections not available to the public (Tampa Bay Museum of Art), behind-the-scenes tours (The Smithsonian), meet-and greets and VIP receptions (Baseball Hall of Fame, which offers such events with baseball legends), access to conference calls with the organization's experts (The Holocaust Museum), and seminars and field trips led by professional experts (scientists, curators, and artists affiliated with Chicago's Field Museum).[35]

Smile Train combines many of these concepts for its top donors who have taken a leadership position in the fight against cleft palate and are part of the organization's Premier Circle. This special group of donors receives personal updates on the organization's

34. http://money.com/money/4133165/nonprofit-donor-rewards/

35. http://money.com/money/4133165/nonprofit-donor-rewards/

programs, VIP invites to special events, special communication and video from the field, the opportunity to travel to partner hospitals around the world, and direct email access to the CEO.[36]

Some nonprofits take a personal approach with their top donors. Rick Allen had participated as a donor for DonorsChoose projects over a number of years. A few years ago, the Founder of the organization, Charles Best, happened to be coming to Charlotte for a talk. The organization reached out to Rick. They invited him to the event and offered to coordinate a short meet and greet after the talk. He took advantage of the offer. A few weeks later, the organization followed up with Rick and suggested that if his travels ever took him to NYC that they would be honored to give him a tour of the headquarters. It just so happened that Rick would be in New York the following week. He did the tour.[37]

The impact of that tactic can be extremely impactful as someone like Rick is going to share that experience with friends and turn it into a powerful story and testimonial for the organization.

Nonprofits themselves need to continue to harness the power of storytelling. "Expect to see storytelling play a much more central role across how nonprofits are building awareness and engaging and influencing donors and stakeholders through marketing. 2019 will also see storytelling being more holistically incorporated across marketing efforts, from brand management, to social media and email marketing, to website design, and annual reports," says David Blyer, CEO, Arreva.[38]

An increasing tactic within storytelling is leveraging the power of data to bring an organization's mission to life. We do this at the Autism MVP Foundation, where our mission focuses on increasing

36. https://www.smiletrain.org/donate/premier-circle

37. Jeanne Allen and http://jeanneallenconsulting.com/

38. Innovation: The Year of Innovation: 40 Nonprofit Trends for 2019 (Nonprofit Pro)

the number and quality of autism-focused educators and therapists. It goes beyond the well-known fact there is a shortage of teachers by sharing powerful data that reinforces why our mission is critical:

1. During the 1980s, the autism diagnosis rate was 1 in 10,000.
2. When my son was born in 2006, the rate was 1 in 88.
3. Later, the rate jumped to 1 in 68, and the latest CDC data reports the rate is 1 in 59.
4. In New Jersey where the foundation is based, the rate is 1 in 34, the highest in the country.[39]

When comparing 1 in 59 and 1 in 34 to the birthrate in the United States, that means approximately 60,000 children are diagnosed with autism nationwide each year, with approximately 3,000 in New Jersey. The math tells you that there simply aren't enough trained professionals to keep up with the demand. By leveraging that data to tell a story, it becomes much more compelling than simply sharing "there is a shortage of autism-focused educators and therapists." These are numbers and facts that are woven into a story around the organization's mission, especially when we announce our annual scholarship winners who are dedicated to a career path to improve educational, social, and daily life skill outcomes for individuals with autism.

Once an individual has taken the important step of making a contribution, donor service is critical. Why? Only 10 percent of donors were very satisfied with the service quality of the organizations they supported, but donors who were very satisfied with service quality were two times more likely to make a further donation than those who were merely satisfied.[40]

39. https://www.cdc.gov/ncbddd/autism/data.html
40. https://www.slideshare.net/blackbaud/back-to-basics-how-to-acquire-retain-and-upgrade-your-donors

LEVERAGING TECHNOLOGY

There are proven ways that technology, and specifically automation, can increase donor satisfaction rates.

Nonprofits can automate and expand the entire process of fundraising with the help of chatbots. Most importantly, this technology makes it possible for an organization to connect with the millions of people who already use messaging platforms like Facebook Messenger and WhatsApp. Your donors and the other people you serve can make requests, complete donations, and keep track of their activity on chatbots quickly and easily. By automating this process, you can make your nonprofit's fundraising efforts hassle-free.[41]

Further, with users expecting shorter response times, it can be tough for any organization to keep up. According to Edison Research, 39 percent of users expect a response on social media within an hour!

However, a chatbot implemented on any messaging platform like Facebook Messenger can help nonprofits quickly and efficiently respond to frequently asked questions through automation. In the long run, this may help your organization reduce people's frustration while also increasing donor and member retention. The faster and better your organization can respond to someone's questions or concerns, the better.[42]

Having phone and email support available to donors can make a huge difference. An analysis of email and phone communication for an annual walk event by a regional branch of a major nonprofit found the following:

> Donors who contacted Support raised an average of $984.51

---

41. http://forums.techsoup.org/cs/community/b/tsblog/archive/2017/08/14/ai-with-a-social-impact-the-top-5-reasons-why-nonprofits-should-explore-chatbots.aspx
42. http://forums.techsoup.org/cs/community/b/tsblog/archive/2017/08/14/ai-with-a-social-impact-the-top-5-reasons-why-nonprofits-should-explore-chatbots.aspx

Donors who did not contact Support raised an average of $194.59[43]

REWARDS AND INCENTIVES

Rewards, incentives, and contests are another proven way to engage donors.

The Pittsburgh Marathon, for example, works with sponsors such as local hotels to donate rooms near the race starting line. In one contest, the marathon's organizers offered racers a chance to win a free room if they raised at least $200 by a certain date. The organizers reported a $9,000 increase in their daily fundraising totals when they activated that promotion.[44]

The Susan B. Komen foundation has provided great incentives for people to raise and donate as much as possible around its races:

- The name of the top fundraising team is printed on the following year's race t-shirts, and the top 20 fundraising team names get listed on Team Captain t-shirts.
- Team Captains whose team raises at least $1,000 receive a pair of earrings. Similarly, team individuals who raise at least $1,000 will receive a pair of earrings.
- Individuals who raise $1,500 or more will receive a Race Day VIP area ticket.
- The top two individuals who raise at least $5,000 win an American Airlines certificate to be redeemed for 25,000

43. https://www.slideshare.net/charitydynamics/participant-support-webinar?qid=d34d8796-4502-4157-95b3-107e8c5dce85&v=&b=&from_search=57
44. https://www.peertopeerforum.com/low-cost-incentives-that-inspire-racers-to-raise-more/

AAdvantage miles that can be redeemed for flights, hotels, upgrades, and shopping.[45]

Finally, it is important to be cognizant of how different donor audiences like to be engaged. For the purpose of simplicity, analyzing donor habits and preferred methods of giving and what inspires to them to give can be broken down by the generations that currently dominate the donor marketplace: Millennials, Gen Xers, and Baby Boomers.[46]

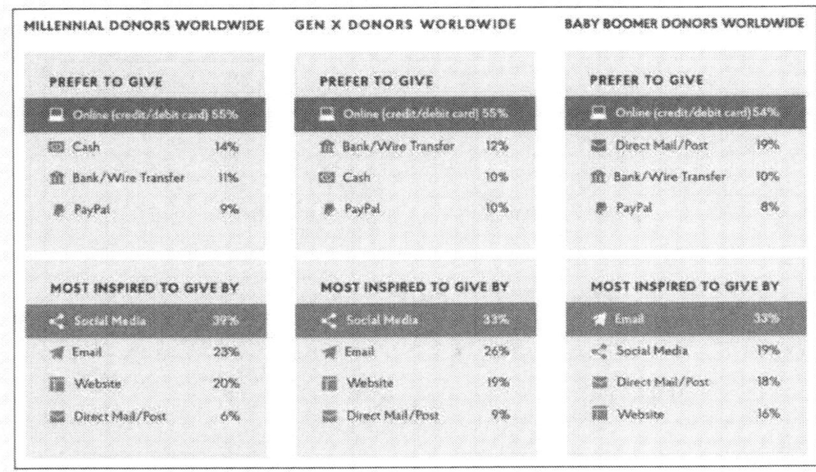

[Source: 2018 Global Trends in Giving Report]

Other interesting takeaways include:

- 31 percent of offline first-time donors are retained for over a year.
- 25 percent of online first-time donors are retained over that same period.

45. https://komenmemorial.org/this-years-race-fundraising-incentives/
46. www.doublethedonation.com

- Online donation pages had a conversion rate of 8 percent.
- The number of conversions via a mobile device increased by 50 percent.[47]
- Further, the average mobile donor gave $79, while the average tablet user gave $96, and desktop user gifted $118.27.
- In terms of email and social engagement, for every 1,000 email addresses, the average nonprofit has 474 Facebook followers, 186 Twitter followers, and 41 Instagram followers.
- Despite the lower Instagram engagement, that was the fasting-growing platform in 2017 with a 44 percent increase in followers.[48]

47. www.doublethedonation.com
48. www.doublethedonation.com

CHAPTER 8

STAFF ENGAGEMENT

"To win in the marketplace you must first win in the workplace."

- Doug Conant

You can't have happy enthused volunteers and donors if you don't have happy engaged staff. Beyond basic compensation, it is important to do the little things to reinforce purpose and drive engagement for team members.

Attitudes begin to form at the initial point of contact with an organization. There is no better place to start thinking about engagement than when you are recruiting and eventually welcoming new staff to your company. Nonprofits derive their strength from dedicated and driven employees, yet according the North Carolina State's *Philanthropy Journal News,* recruitment and retention remain a high or moderate challenge for 6 in 10 nonprofit leaders.

Smart nonprofits take advantage of these early days in order to ensure a strong, productive, and dedicated workforce. "The way you manage the transition of somebody into your culture speaks volumes about the culture to the person coming in, because you're making those first early impressions and they know what's expected of them," says George Bradt, Managing Director at PrimeGenesis.[49]

RECRUITING AND ONBOARDING

With for-profit companies increasing their sense of purpose through well-defined and meaningful CSR initiatives, this is putting a greater demand on nonprofits to compete for employees who want "giving back" to be part of their daily work experience. So, what can they do? Here are some changes nonprofits can make.

According to the Society of Human Resource Management, 64 percent of nonprofits do not have a formal recruitment strategy and 70 percent reported that they have no formal recruitment budget. A whopping 81 percent have no formal retention strategy. About 70 percent have not developed an employment brand, despite the

49. https://primegenesis.com/

important role branding plays in attracting top talent. Only 33 percent of nonprofits said they use an applicant tracking system or candidate relationship management platform—tools that can make recruiting more efficient and improve the candidate experience.

Onboarding is a bright spot, however, with 63 percent of nonprofits saying they have a formal onboarding process and 31 percent reporting that they use an informal process." Here's how the formal transition or onboarding process for new staff is defined:

> Onboarding, also known as organizational socialization, refers to the mechanism through which new employees acquire the necessary knowledge, skills, and behaviors to become effective organizational members and insiders. Tactics used in this process include formal meetings, lectures, videos, printed materials, or computer-based orientations to introduce newcomers to their new jobs and organizations.[50]

Unfortunately, less than 25 percent of organizations have a formal onboarding process. According to onboarding pioneer and expert George Bradt, "Most organizations haven't thought things through in advance. On their first day, they [e.g., new recruits] are welcomed by such confidence-building remarks as: Oh, you're here. We'd better find you an office."

WHY IS ONBOARDING CRITICAL?

Research shows that employees make the critical decision to stay or leave within the first six months of joining an organization. When new hires participate in an onboarding program, the nonprofit can "maximize retention, engagement, and productivity."[51] Socialization

50. https://en.wikipedia.org/wiki/Onboarding
51. https://www.scribd.com/document/260057030/Onboarding-Toolkit-for-HR-Professionals

efforts lead to positive outcomes for new staff, including higher job satisfaction, better job performance, greater organizational commitment, and reduction in stress.

Yet, culturally onboarding new staff can be a real challenge. While sleek videos, laminated pocket cards, and lobby placards may help staff memorize the values, the actual understanding of how to "live" the nonprofit values can be a whole other story. Your culture is only as cohesive as the people willing to live out the shared values. Actions speak louder than words.

Having a diverse range of ways to welcome a new hire is critical to establishing a healthy employer-employee relationship. Here's an example of a nonprofit that purposefully goes the extra mile to engage new staff members:

Community Links is an award-winning nonprofit provider of mental health and wellbeing services in Yorkshire, England. According to the "Best Companies" website,[52] new employees at Community Links get:

- one-to-one meetings with the CEO and senior management team
- support from a more experienced colleague
- encouragement to develop leadership skills through shadowing

TRANSPARENCY

Transparency and openness in the nonprofit workplace is vital. Vineet Nayar, former CEO of HCL Technologies, touched on trust

52. https://www.b.co.uk/company-profile/?community-links-53640

in his bestselling book, *Employees First, Customers Second.*[53] In the book, he outlined four ways that transparency builds trust:

1. Transparency ensures that every stakeholder knows the company's vision and understands how their contribution assists the organization in achieving its goals. Working in an environment without transparency is like trying to solve a jigsaw puzzle without knowing what the finished picture is supposed to look like.

2. It ensures that every stakeholder has a deep personal commitment to the aims of the organization.

3. Millennial and Gen Z members expect transparency as a given. They post their life stories in public domains; they expect nothing less in their workplaces.

4. In a knowledge economy, we want customers to be transparent with us, to share their ideas, their vision, and their strategies for solving core problems. Why would customers be transparent with us if we don't trust employees enough to be transparent with them?

MissionBox recommends creating a compensation structure to promote transparency. This structure translates your compensation philosophy into a cash equivalent. According to an article on the company's website,[54] it is a best practice to state the salary ranges and benefits for all staff positions, including detailed job descriptions, required levels of education and experience, and schedules for salary adjustments. They recommend to document the process used to create your compensation structure. For transparency, "describe the data you used and who was involved in these decisions, as well

53. http://www.forbes.com/sites/karlmoore/2012/05/14/employees-first-customers-second-why-it-really-works-in-the-market/
54. https://www.missionbox.com/article/144/employee-compensation-best-practices-for-nonprofits

as when the compensation structure was created and how often it'll be reviewed and updated."

Here is an example of how to instill transparency. Community Links has a birthday afternoon tea with senior managers to improve communication. The program has bred trust and connected employees to the overall vision of the organization. One day a month, senior management work from different sites, which increases engagement between employees and makes the senior team more approachable.[55]

TEAM BUILDING

Success is frequently seen as a purely individual achievement, often at the expense of others. But in the nonprofit world, an organization can only thrive with the collective help of everyone. For staff, being part of a team helps create a sense of belonging. Feeling more connected leads to a greater level of happiness.

Let's look at three nonprofits who actively foster a sense of community through team building.

Kiva is a nonprofit whose mission is to connect people and alleviate poverty by facilitating microloans, enabling individuals to lend as little as $25 to help create opportunity around the world. Staff members receive free massages, yoga, snacks, paid trips to visit Kiva's partners in the field, and a monthly recess where employees indulge in playtime. "The spirit of having fun and really caring about each other and encouraging each other is what makes Kiva such an incredible place to work," says Jackie Bernstein, Product Manager.[56]

Newydd Housing Association stresses the importance of well-being. The organization has a health and wellbeing group called InShape

55. https://www.b.co.uk/company-profile/?community-links-53640

56. https://www.themuse.com/advice/10-nonprofits-employees-love-to-work-for

that has a dedicated budget and meets quarterly. Activities have included group bike rides, lunchtime walks, art classes, knitting, craft sessions, yoga, and tap-dance classes. There are stress-management training sessions, subsidized massages, and communal bikes.[57]

Bay Area-based nonprofit Downtown Streets Team wanted their employees to feel so good they created a committee dedicated to it! The Feel Good Committee organizes events for the organization, such as beach days, barbecues, and the annual holiday party. The committee once organized a joint wedding shower for four employees getting married that summer. That would make anyone feel good![58]

RECOGNITION

Reaching the heart of your employees involves recognition. In the words of Angela Maiers, "YOU MATTER. These two words can change your mood, change your mind, and have the power to change lives and the world if we understand and leverage them in the right way."[59]

Recognition resonates in the workplace. Thirty-five percent of workers and 30 percent of chief financial officers cited frequent recognition of accomplishments as the most effective non-monetary reward. Thanking people for their hard work and commitment is key to making them feel appreciated.[60]

Recognition fuels a sense of worth and belonging in individuals. No rocket science here, as humans we crave acceptance. Dale Carnegie spoke of the importance of recognition more than 80 years ago.

57. https://www.b.co.uk/company-profile/?newydd-housing-association-90131
58. https://beni.fit/nonprofits-making-employee-recognition-priceless-benefit/
59. http://www.angelamaiers.com/2011/08/new-ted-talk-you-matter.html
60. http://accountemps.rhi.mediaroom.com/index.php?s=189&item=213

Here are a couple of quotes from his classic, *How to Win Friends and Influence People.*[61]

"Be lavish in your praise and hearty in your approbation."

And the often paraphrased, "A drop of honey gathers more bees than a gallon of gall [vinegar]."

Most managers take an "if, then" approach to recognizing staff members. Shawn Achor believes this paradigm needs to change "from thinking that encouragement and recognition should be used as rewards for high performance . . . to thinking that encouragement and recognition are drivers of high performance."[62]

Let's have a look at four companies who give a little extra when it comes to employee recognition.

Regenda Homes is a housing association owning and managing over 13,000 properties in England. Regenda offers spot awards to reward employees who have gone the "extra mile." The awards have been given for resolving a customer complaint, working extra hours, and delivering a successful project. Managers and team members can nominate team members and colleagues to be presented with pay bonuses.[63]

Reginald Hughes is a vice president at Goodwill of Lower South Carolina—a nonprofit agency employing people with disabilities—He knows that nurturing healthy work environments is essential to building more productive employees. "Feeling appreciated is a morale booster. I've seen it firsthand," he says.

Hughes is part of a team of staff that helped create an employee rewards and recognition program at its Charleston work site. The program

61. https://www.amazon.com/How-Win-Friends-Influence-People/dp/0671027034
62. https://www.amazon.com/Happiness-Advantage-Positive-Brain-Success/dp/0307591557
63. https://www.b.co.uk/company-profile/?regenda-limited-53283

relies on management and supervisors to regularly nominate standout staff for their hard work and dedication. Following a monthly review of nominations, Goodwill management personally gifts company promotional items such as baseball caps, mugs, and pins to deserving employees. Even members of Congress who visit and tour Goodwill's work sites have participated in the gifting process.

Hughes said because Goodwill's employee rewards and recognition program was so successful at its Charleston work site, he wanted to expand it to additional Goodwill locations.

"The employee rewards and recognition program at our Charleston work site has helped us highlight the great work of our employees with disabilities and build advocates on their behalf," Hughes said. "By expanding it to our other locations in South Carolina, we knew we could connect more employees to the larger company and the mission. We believe programs like this should exist in every workplace. Goodwill is proud to create an environment where employees can be recognized and thrive."[64]

The Kaleidoscope Plus Group is a health and wellbeing charity that works with people of all ages with a particular focus on mental health. Their mission is to promote and support positive health and wellbeing with the ultimate aim of providing services on a national level. The Employee Recognition Awards program highlights individuals who have gone above and beyond the call of duty. They get a certificate and a free place at the annual gala ball, gift vouchers, or two tickets to a football match. Employee of the Year gets free accommodation for a week away in Cyprus.[65]

Melin Homes has a "Diloch" (thank you in Welsh) program. As well as offering rewards through vouchers, flowers, lunch, and afternoon tea, Diolch encourages staff to show appreciation to each

64. https://www.sourceamerica.org/stories/grant-enables-nonprofit-enhance-employee-recognition-program

65. https://www.b.co.uk/company-profile/?the-kaleidoscope-plus-group-93682

other through messages. Recipients get certificates, chocolates, a tree planting, or a charity donation.[66]

ESTABLISHING A CULTURE OF LEARNING

Investing in your staff involves training and development. Let's look at three nonprofits that go the extra mile to allow staff to learn how to become the best version of themselves.

Regenda Homes has the LEAD program. LEAD offers participants the chance to work-shadow, learn new skills, and showcase talent to senior managers. Employees have become involved in projects they otherwise wouldn't have the opportunity to be part of, have attended the CIH conference and Young Leaders Conference, and benefited from mentoring opportunities.[67]

The Transformation Unit is a National Health Service (NHS) internal consultancy based in Manchester, England. They provide consultancy services to the public sector based around strategic transformation and planning, finance and analytics, project and program management, and organizational strategy and engagement. Under their Calibration Process, everyone completes a health and wellbeing plan, a contribution framework, and talent plan. The Transformation Academy also offers timed placements and experiences outside people's normal roles. It offers targeted development so individuals can move into their aspirational job role. In a survey of TU staff, 100 percent of staff agreed to the statement, "The experience I gain from this job is valuable for my future."[68]

Fair Ways is a nonprofit that delivers a comprehensive range of services to children and young people, including social care, support,

---

66. https://www.b.co.uk/company-profile/?melin-homes-54341
67. https://www.b.co.uk/company-profile/?53283
68. https://www.b.co.uk/company-profile/?transformation-unit-106940

training, and education services. Fair Ways promotes staff learning by offering regular drop-in master classes. The organization also makes external coaches available alongside mentoring from the senior team and also offers away days. Staff are given a Career Passport which provides examples of good working practice and training required to progress at the organization. The organization offers a one-year Future Leaders Program that focuses on the skills and experience for more senior roles. Staff members can also apply for a £10,000 Education Grant.[69]

EMPOWERMENT

Leadership is about inspiring others. It's enabling staff members to do their absolute best to work toward a meaningful and rewarding shared purpose. In one word—EMPOWERMENT. Help people find their direction, support them with resources, and then get out of their way.

Command and Control thinking is outdated. People do not enjoy or appreciate being controlled or coerced. The best managers figure out how to get great outcomes by setting the appropriate context rather than by trying to control their people.[70]

According to Ken and Scott Blanchard, "We are finding that giving people a chance to succeed in their job and setting them free to a certain degree is the key to motivation as opposed to trying to direct and control people's energy. It's really about letting go and connecting people to their work—and each other—rather than channeling, organizing, orchestrating, and focusing behavior."[71]

---

69. https://www.b.co.uk/company-profile/?fair-ways-101878
70. http://www.slideshare.net/reed2001/culture-1798664
71. http://www.fastcompany.com/3002382/why-trying-manipulate-employee-motivation-always-backfires

CHAPTER 9

BOARD ENGAGEMENT

"People are yearning to be asked to use the full measure of their potential for something they care about."

- Dan Pallotta

Having a dedicated, experienced, and engaged board is critical upon launching a nonprofit and key to enjoying sustained success. In fact, any nonprofit in the US must identify its board members when filing an initial application with the IRS.

Given that most nonprofit board members are volunteers, it can be no small task to keep a board engaged and a nonprofit running smoothly. With busy, professional, full-time careers, family lives, and other interests, nearly any nonprofit board member will be stretched thin. Therefore, it is critical to give board members a defined role in the organization and remind them how valuable their contributions are to the enterprise.

One of the best ways to engage a board and keep it active is to involve them in the strategic planning process. This "roadmap to success" will help set the course for an organization and should be revisited every few years or so. Honest opinions of the "good, bad, and the ugly" are necessary in order for the organization to succeed and move forward. A board is an important part of this process, but donors, volunteers, staff, sponsors, and other partner organizations also play a key role.

Taking a step back on the board side, a common tactic to engage board members is through a retreat, which can (and should be) led by an outside facilitator, and feature a detailed agenda and fun activities.

Here are some common themes and ways to make a board retreat successful:

1. The purpose of the retreat has to be clear.

2. Each board member should feel a sense of ownership of the success of the retreat.[72]

72. https://www.joangarry.com/board-retreat/

3. The work must (begin to) come to life at the retreat.[73]

4. Next to the agenda, the location of the retreat is the most important aspect.[74]

5. Have a set course of action, with timelines, to follow up on the action items from the retreat.

There are other elements that can help make a retreat successful, including icebreakers and other fun activities, and more importantly, spending the time to find the right facilitator. Following up on the agenda and driving action from the meeting is critical. All too often retreats happen with the best intentions only for all of the time and hard work to go to waste because there isn't proper follow up on the action items. The best of intentions often go by the wayside.

Nonprofit consultant Joan Garry in her "Goosebump a Week" solution to reengage board members notes at its root, the idea is about storytelling, and is simple and effective.

The story should be:

- True
- Current
- Personal
- Mission centric
- Easy to retell
- Easy to remember (sticky)

---

73. https://www.joangarry.com/board-retreat/

74. https://quickbooks.intuit.com/ca/resources/nonprofit-organizations/board-retreats-non-profit/

- Give your board members at least one goosebump
- Impactful for the organization and as clear as day[75]

According to Garry, board members will now be more engaged and be better equipped to tell an organization's story once they read a brief anecdote that provides goosebumps. And once that story is tied back to the mission of the organization, board members suddenly have a powerful and memorable way to share the impact on the people it serves.

Another key way to engage a board is to install a customized method of tracking how your board members engage with the organization. The tracking could become part of regular board discussions and categorized like this:[76]

GIVING

- Gift in past 12 months
- Multiple year/recurring (monthly, quarterly) gifts
- Employer gift/matching
- Identifying potential donors/supporters
- Bequest indicated

PARTICIPATION

- Board & committee meeting attendance
- Attending events

75. https://www.joangarry.com/keep-board-members-engaged/
76. https://www.slideshare.net/bloomerang/everything-you-need-to-know-about-increasing-donor-and-board-member-engagement?qid=77a68be8-d83d-4481-b4b3-a8cfe2289c9e&v=&b=&from_search=12

- Volunteering
- Active in leadership role
- Active participation in board discussions
- Recommending board member candidates

COMMUNICATION

- How they engage with or promote the enterprise via Facebook, LinkedIn, social media
- Responsiveness to board work through e-mail or board portal

CHAPTER 10

THE EIGHT PURPOSE ARCHETYPES

"Everything a brand does—from stores to product to packaging to how you feel about that brand—has to be designed."

- Lee Clow, TBWAChiatDay/Los Angeles

We began the *Red Goldfish Project* in 2015. Since its inception, we've collected information on over 250 companies, specifically looking for ways that organizations bring their purpose to life. Our research database includes over 700 articles and nearly 3,500 videos. [See the collection of videos searchable by brand, archetype, and chapter at http://602communications.com/RedGoldfish]

In reviewing all of the companies, we began to see patterns. We saw that organizations would typically fall into one of eight purpose archetypes:

1. **The Protector** - Those who protect what is important

   Example: The Nature Conservancy is dedicated to solving our planet's biggest challenges, including tackling climate change, protecting land and water, providing food and water sustainability, and building health cities.[77]

2. **The Liberator** - Those who reinvent a broken system

   Example: Donors Choose helps mitigate the absurdity of already underpaid public school teachers paying for school supplies and other classroom materials out of their pockets. The organization aim is to "make it easy for anyone to help a classroom in need, moving us closer to a nation where students in every community have the tools and experiences they need for a great education."[78]

3. **The Designer** - Those who empower through the creation of revolutionary products.

---

77. https://www.nature.org/en-us/what-we-do/our-priorities/

78. https://www.donorschoose.org/about

Example: The nonprofit 3dp4me.org's mission is to serve real human needs through practical 3-D printing. The company's first project is to provide 12,000 hearing aids over five years to refugees and low-income clients in Jordan.[79]

4. **The Guide** - Those who help facilitate individual progress

   Example: Self Help International's mission is to alleviate hunger by helping people help themselves. They assist the rural poor and small-scale farmers in developing countries. They help them become self-reliant in meeting the needs of families and communities through training, education, leadership development, and other forms of assistance.[80]

5. **The Advocate** - Those who advocate for a tribe

   Example: Autism treatment for children can be costly and certain therapies are not covered by insurance or worse, are not offered by some school districts thanks to archaic state laws and clueless politicians. The online Autism Treatment Center program offers an affordable, in-home alternative for parents or caregivers to help students with autism reach their maximum potential.[81]

6. **The Challenger** - Those who inspire people toward transformative action

   Example: The mission of DREAMers Roadmap is "to inspire more students to enroll in college knowing that

79. https://www.3dp4me.org/
80. https://www.selfhelpinternational.org/our-mission/
81. https://online.autismtreatmentcenter.org/

there is a tool to help them find financial resources quickly and easily."[82]

7. **The Unifier** - Those who command individuals to join a movement

   Example: The nonprofit 80,000 Hours helps people choose a career that will have a social impact. This is from their website: An individual has approximately 80,000 hours in a career. Choose how you spend that time well, and you can have a hugely positive impact on the world. Choose badly, and you might not make any difference at all outside your own family or organization. We're here to give you the information you need to maximize the social impact of your career choices. Our advice is based on four years of research with academics at Oxford and is tailored for talented young graduates. We're a nonprofit, so it's all independent and free."[83]

8. **The Master** - Those on a mission to change lives and improve the world

   Example: Apps for Good is an educational technology movement transforming the way technology is taught in schools, aiming to turn young tech consumers into tech creators. Apps for Good strives to utilize the confidence and talent of our next generation of problem solvers and digital makers, youth who are ready to tackle the 21st century workplace and are enthusiastic about creating new tech ideas that can change the world for the better.[84]

---

82. https://www.ffwd.org/tech-nonprofits/s/dreamers-roadmap/
83. https://www.ffwd.org/tech-nonprofits/s/80000-hours/
84. https://www.ffwd.org/tech-nonprofits/s/apps-for-good/

HIERARCHY OF NEEDS

The order for the eight archetypes is meaningful. We were inspired by Abraham Maslow's hierarchy of human needs. Maslow presented the hierarchy in his 1943 paper entitled, "A Theory of Human Motivation" in *Psychological Review.* The five-stage pyramid model goes from basic needs to psychological needs. At the top of the pyramid is sell-fulfillment. Here is how we see our eight archetypes within the Maslow framework:

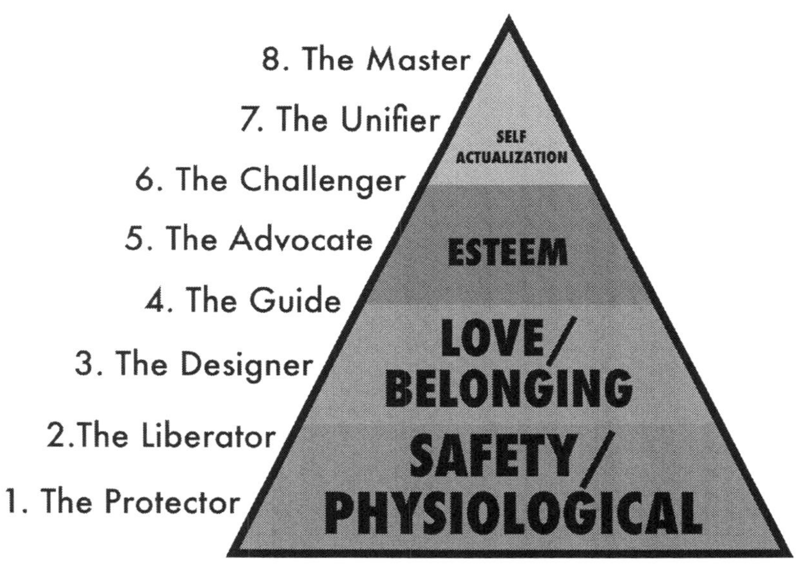

Let's now jump into the first of the eight archetypes: The Protector.

The Protector

The first archetype is The Protector. The purpose of The Protector is rooted in Maslow's concept of safety. The goal is to protect what is important.

The symbol of The Protector is Superman. Nonprofits with The Protector archetype are motivated to help others and their surroundings. In the words of the Man of Steel, "The welfare of Earth and all its people will always be my primary concern. But if there is a solution for hunger, it must be one that comes from the compassionate heart of man and extends outward toward his fellow man. To reach out to those in need and inspire others to do the same. That is life's greatest necessity and its most precious gift."

The Liberator

The second archetype is The Liberator. The purpose of The Liberator is rooted in Maslow's concept of safety. The goal is to liberate and help others by reinventing a broken system and striving to help others break away from bondage.

The symbol of The Liberator is Moses. Brands with The Liberator archetype are motivated to do things differently, leading others to a better place. In the words of Moses, "All who thirst for freedom may come with us. Tomorrow the light of freedom will shine upon us as we go forth from Egypt."

The Designer

The third archetype is The Designer. The purpose of The Designer is rooted in Maslow's concept of safety and love. The goal is to empower others through the creation of revolutionary products.

The symbol of The Designer is Doc Brown. Brands with The Designer archetype are creators. They persist in building stylish products that change the world. They are wired to push through adversity. In the words of Doc Brown from *Back to the Futu*re, "The way I see it, if you're gonna build a time machine into a car, why not do it with some style?"

The Guide

The fourth archetype is The Guide. The purpose of The Guide is rooted in Maslow's concept of love. The goal is to help facilitate individual progress.

The symbol of The Guide is Mr. Miyagi from the movie *The Karate Kid.* Nonprofits with The Guide archetype are teachers. They want to help others navigate the world. They are wired to educate. In the words of Mr. Miyagi after Daniel asked if he could teach him the crane technique, "First learn stand, then learn fly. Nature rule, Daniel-san, not mine."

The Advocate

The fifth archetype is The Advocate. The purpose of The Advocate is rooted in Maslow's concept of love. The goal is to help advocate for a tribe.

The symbol of The Advocate is Atticus Finch from *To Kill A Mockingbird.* Nonprofits with The Advocate archetype are passionate supporters. They want to stand up for certain groups of people in this world. They are wired to fight. In the words of the lawyer Atticus Finch, "You'll decide you don't like the taste of injustice, not for you and not for anyone, and you'll understand that even though all the battles can't be won, that doesn't mean you won't fight."

The Challenger

The sixth archetype is The Challenger. The purpose of The Challenger is rooted in Maslow's concepts of love and esteem. The goal is to inspire individuals to take individual action.

The symbol of The Challenger is Maximus from *Gladiator*. Nonprofits with The Challenger archetype seek to become change agents. They want to inspire individuals to become a better version of themselves. In the words of Maximus, "Three weeks from now, I will be harvesting my crops. Imagine where you will be, and it will be so. Hold the line! Stay with me! If you find yourself alone, riding in the green fields with the sun on your face, do not be troubled. For you are in Elysium, and you're already dead! [Cavalry laughs] Brothers, what we do in life . . . echoes in eternity."

The Unifier

The seventh archetype is The Unifier. The purpose of The Unifier is rooted in Maslow's concepts of esteem and self-actualization. The goal is to command individuals to join a movement.

The symbol of The Unifier is Scottish freedom fighter William Wallace from the movie *Braveheart*. Brands with The Unifier archetype seek to lead others. They want to set the future standard. In the words of William Wallace, "Help me. In the name of Christ, help yourselves. Now is our chance. Now. If we join, we can win. If we win, well then we'll have what none of us has ever had before: a country of our own."

The Master

The eighth archetype is The Master. The purpose of The Master is rooted in Maslow's concept of self-actualization. The goal is to change lives toward transcendence.

The symbol of The Master is Yoda from *Star Wars*. Brands with The Master archetype seek to improve the world. They want to set the future standard. In the words of Yoda, "Always two there are, no more, no less. A master and an apprentice."

PART III:

CREATING YOUR OWN ENGAGEMENT IDEAS

CHAPTER 11

THE I.D.E.A. PROCESS

"No matter what people tell you, words and ideas can change the world."

- Robin Williams

Since the release of *Purple Goldfish* in 2012, we've trained hundreds of companies and organizations. As you might imagine, it's not enough to help an organization understand what a Goldfish is and why they need them, organizations also need help creating their own Goldfish, so we developed the I.D.E.A. Process.

Here's the overview of the I.D.E.A. Process:

Inquire – understand what is important to your stakeholders and what gaps and opportunities exist in their journey.

Design – generate ideas for Red Goldfish to address the gaps and opportunities in your current customer journey.

Evaluate – complete internal analysis and external pilot to determine which Red Goldfish, or RGF (Red Goldfish Fry) for short, should be rolled out across the organization.

Advance – bring your best RGFs out of the pilot phase and into widespread rollout, measuring the results, and creating a feedback loop back to the Inquire phase.

In the next four chapters we'll walk you through the steps of the I.D.E.A. Process.

CHAPTER 12

INQUIRE

"A subtle thought that is in error may yet give rise to fruitful inquiry that can establish truths of great value."

- Isaac Asimov

Inquire is to ask questions to find direction. During the Inquire phase you're going to ask lots of questions of both people and data.

Before you undertake the creation of a Red Goldfish, you must first understand the big picture, something experience professionals call the customer journey. By understanding your volunteer and donor journeys, and that no two are alike, you can discover the gaps and opportunities to create Red Goldfish. Let's start by learning more about journeys, gaps, and opportunities.

JOURNEYS

As the name implies, a journey is everything your stakeholders experience as they interact with your nonprofit before, during, and after. Think for a moment about the last time you used a hotel. Could you list every interaction you had with the hotel before, during, and after your purchase? If you could, your list might look something like this:

- Decide to take a trip
- Research places to stay
- Select an area of town
- Look for hotel options
- Compare hotels
- Select a hotel
- Compare hotel rooms
- Book a hotel room

- Travel to your destination
- Locate your hotel
- Enter the lobby
- Wait for a front desk clerk
- Check in
- Find your room
- Open the door
- Walk inside
- Stay one or more nights
- Check out of your room
- And then travel back home
- Tell others about your experience

This might seem like a long list but it only scratches the surface of what steps a donor or volunteer might take in their journey with your nonprofit. Experience professionals would call each of these steps a touchpoint, and we study touchpoints on what we call a journey map, but before we create journey maps, we need to gather insights about our stakeholders.

STAKEHOLDER INSIGHTS

There isn't a right way to gather stakeholder insights, but there are plenty of wrong ways. Let's start with the most common one. It sounds something like this: "We've been doing this at our nonprofit for thirty years. We know exactly what our stakeholders want." Cue the dramatic music. The biggest trap you can fall into is assuming you know exactly what your stakeholders want. Sure, you likely have a good sense of their needs, but there's always so much more you can learn.

There are entire books on gathering insights, so we won't try to recreate that here, but what we will offer are some thoughts on the best sources of stakeholder insight. As you prepare to map their journey, you want to answer the following questions:

- What do our volunteers and donors care about? Which one thing do they care about most?
- What do volunteers and donors expect from similar organizations?
- How well do we meet their expectations today?
- What are common points of failure for us?

As you seek to answer these questions, there are numerous sources of input that may be helpful. Here are a few that we suggest our clients turn to:

- Data – What data does your organization gather that might provide insights into your volunteers and donors? Also, how does your CRM allow you to utilize that information and where are the shortfalls?
- Surveys – Do you conduct any volunteer and donor surveys, including Net Promoter or Customer Effort scores?
- External data – Are external data or reports available about your volunteer and donor segments?
- Interviews – Can you sit down and interview a sample of your volunteers and donors?

- Observations – Can you observe volunteer and donor interactions either in-person or via recordings?

Often experience Professionals Those who track the donor experience for nonprofits will document insights about a stakeholder in a document called a persona. Personas are profiles of prototypical stakeholders based on actual data. Often these personas will be organized by the type of stakeholder. For instance, a nonprofit might have different personas for volunteers, donors, and staff to name a few of their key audiences.

In our workshops, we often create proto-personas. These are persona-like documents that allow our participants to get the feel of creating personas but are often based on their personal experiences and not on stakeholder data. Proto-personas can be helpful for training or for creating a first draft of personas but must be validated by data to be useful.

Personas are great at documenting what your stakeholders want, but often do not include how well you perform against their desires. For that exercise, we often create an Attribute Map. An Attribute Map is a graph where you list your stakeholder's needs on one side in rank order and then rate your relative performance on a scale of 1-5 (1 is worst, 5 is best). Here's an example:

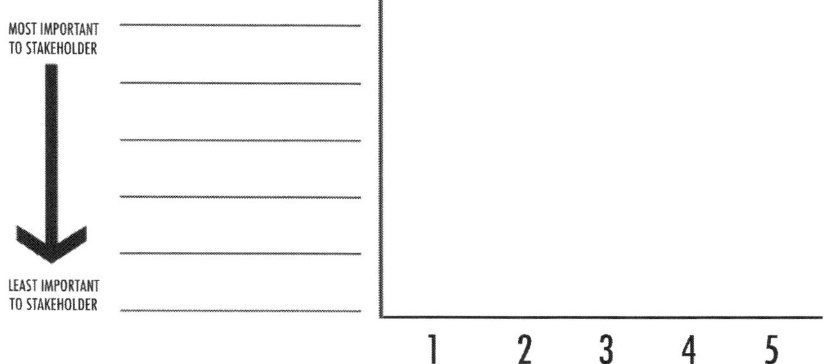

As you can see, the map clearly shows what your customers need and where you fall short. This high-level exercise can help you decide where to focus your experience design efforts or can inform the journey mapping process in the next step.

Armed with insight, either in its raw form or organized into personas, you now know what your volunteers and donors want and expect. The Attribute Map and other data about your current performance give you the raw insights that will help you document their journey in step two and then identify gaps and opportunities in step three.

INQUIRE PHASE PROGRESS

✓	**Step One:** Gather Customer Insight
	Step Two: Create Journey Maps
	Step Three: Identify Gaps and Opportunities

JOURNEY MAPS

Journey maps are designed to create a sense of empathy. By looking at all of your touchpoints, good, bad, and ugly, all on one document, you can step into the shoes of your volunteers and donors and feel their pain or delight. Of course, the latter is what ~~we're~~ we are going for.

In our workshops, we encourage participants to create both current state and future state journey maps. The current state documents what is happening today, while the future state is the journey you might aspire to create.

You can choose to create a high-level journey map that covers all steps of the volunteer or donor journey but with less detail or you can choose to create a detailed map for a specific segment of the journey to help you perfect a critical part of the journey.

Journey maps do not have to be exhaustive. In fact, it's easy to get caught up on creating the most exhaustive journey map possible. We believe this takes your focus away from actually solving your stakeholder challenges or worse causes you to miss the proverbial forest for the trees.

Often in our workshops, we ask participants to organize their journey maps in rows by the touchpoint's medium as different touchpoints happen via social media, via the web, or in-person events.

There are a number of great resources out there on journey mapping, so we won't seek to reinvent that wheel here, but getting back to our original hotel example, here's a list of journey maps a hotel might choose to create and how each could be useful.

- **The booking experience** – a detailed journey map including all of the steps needed to book a room, divided by channel, which includes social media, the hotel website, the call center, travel agents, and travel booking websites. This map looks for gaps and opportunities to streamline and simplify the booking process. a detailed journey map including all of the steps needed to make a donation, divided by channel, which includes social media, the website, mail order via a brochure or in-person communication. This map looks for gaps and opportunities to streamline and simplify the booking process.

- **The in-room experience** – a detailed map of the things a guest might choose to do from their guestroom and the related touchpoints. This map could include making coffee, using the iron, and ordering room service. This map is to make improvements to facilities, amenities, or guest services. a detailed map of the things a donor might be able to do during and after making the donation. This map could include the user experience via a third-party payment processor (including receipt acknowledgement, what choices the donor could make and the type of interaction once redirected after the online donation, and how and how quickly a "thank you" is provided. This map is to make improvements to the process, analyze the speed and ease for the donor, and perhaps even measure how the felt about the donor experience from start to finish.

- **The high-level experience** – a not-so-detailed map of every phase of the guest's journey with the hotel with external factors included. This might resemble the list earlier in this chapter. Some external factors might include a flight delay, transportation services to the hotel, or other travel irritation. This map is to help staff have greater empathy for the guest and look for opportunities to improve the guest's trip, even if the hotel didn't cause the underlying issue. a not-so-detailed map of every phase of the donor's journey. Some external factors might include a slow processing of a payment, load time for the website, the contents of the acknowledgement and subsequent "thank you." This map is to help staff have greater empathy for the donor and look for opportunities to improve the donor's giving journey.

There are all sorts of ways to approach journey mapping and there's no right answer, except that you must consider two factors:

1. Does the journey map give you enough detail to understand how you might improve the volunteer and donor experience?

2. Is the journey map based on actual insights from your volunteers and donors, data about them, or insights from your front-line employees?

If the answer to those questions is anything other than a confident yes, you likely need to adjust your approach.

INQUIRE PHASE PROGRESS

✓	**Step One:** Gather Customer Insight
✓	**Step Two:** Create Journey Maps
	Step Three: Identify Gaps and Opportunities

GAPS AND OPPORTUNITIES

A few times during this chapter we've mentioned gaps and opportunities. Now it's time for us to talk more about those.

A gap in your volunteer or donor journey is a failure or a breakdown. These are points along the journey where your nonprofit processes get in the way of their goal or do not serve their needs. The result is often frustration.

Unexpected cases of stakeholder frustration can occur as well. Journey mapping helps you minimize these cases, but they always will exist, so create an "issue resolution" journey map to plan how you might handle the occasional misstep or mistake. These one-off mistakes aren't what we mean by gaps. Gaps are systemic breakdowns in your stakeholder experience.

As you review your journey map, think of gaps as valleys or potholes. These are the parts of the stakeholder experience you want to address. Speaking of potholes, let's use a roadway analogy for a moment.

Let's say that your stakeholder journey resembles a road that is flat and straight, and you've pointed out several potholes. Suppose you use all of your budget to fill every pothole, but you still have a road that's flat and straight. While there are no issues riding down your road, there's also not much excitement.

Now envision a curvy mountain road—the kind of road where motorists will travel from afar to experience. There are twists, turns, views, and any number of hazards that create a thrill. Let's say that there are also a fair number of potholes.

Which road would you rather experience? The perfectly maintained but boring pavement or the exciting but imperfect one? We suspect it's the latter.

In the *Power of Moments,* Chip and Dan Heath caution against using all of your resources to address gaps. They advocate for the creation of peak moments. That is investing in experiences that are memorable and stand out.

Gaps are easy to find and easy to spend all of your time chasing. If you do that, however, you'll engage in a never-ending game of Whack-A-Mole and never create an experience that is remarkable. We encourage you to address your largest gaps but also spend time identifying the opportunities to create a peak moment. Some of the best Red Goldfish create peak moments for volunteers and donors.

Identifying opportunities is much more difficult than looking for gaps. Opportunities can exist in a gap. For instance, you could choose to double down on a common gap in your industry not only to solve it but to turn it into a peak experience.

For the most part, however, your opportunities won't come from gaps. They will come from ordinary experiences. We ask our workshop participants to review their journey maps for ordinary moments that might resonate with their stakeholders. Using an example from the for-profit world, an example of this comes from

The Durham Hotel in Durham, North Carolina. The retro-chic boutique hotel is a haven for today's modern consumer. The property features a gourmet coffee bar and a lavish rooftop patio, not to mention well-designed, modern guestrooms. Knowing that their hotel attracts a foodie audience, they decided to transform the in-room coffee experience. A coffee pot is a staple of most US hotel rooms. Most hotels purchase filter packs of Starbucks or another recognized coffee brand and ensure rooms are well-stocked. Some hotels take it to the next level with an in-room Keurig and a selection of K-cups.

The Durham, however, takes a different approach. Each guestroom has a door hanger that resembles a breakfast room service menu, except that at The Durham the card lists a choice of beans from Durham-based Counter Culture, one of the top five craft roasters in the country. The card allows you to select your beans and the time of day when you would like for your freshly ground coffee to be delivered. Oh, and did we mention that the coffee service is complimentary? In the morning, by your chosen time, you'll have a sealed packet of your freshly-ground coffee choice waiting for you outside your door. Talk about a "perk."

Before creating this experience, we're certain that The Durham didn't see coffee as a gap. Their guests are generally not expecting a gourmet, in-room coffee experience, but it was an opportunity to create a peak moment.

How does this translate to the nonprofit world? What is a peak experience for a volunteer? As a docent at a museum, it could be creating an easier connection with the visitor.

Now that we've completed the Inquiry stage, it's time to start creating Red Goldfish. Let's move into the Design phase of the I.D.E.A. Process.

INQUIRE PHASE PROGRESS

✓	**Step One:** Gather Customer Insight
✓	**Step Two:** Create Journey Maps
✓	**Step Three:** Identify Gaps and Opportunities

CHAPTER 13

DESIGN

"Design is not just what it looks like and feels like.
Design is how it works."

— Steve Jobs

Design is the most exciting part of the I.D.E.A. Process. It's where you generate ideas, some of which may very well be innovative, to better serve your volunteers, donors, and staff. Ideation is rarely a linear process. Some ideas come from an epiphany and others build on each other.

While ideas come to us when we least expect it, there are ways to organize the ideation process and that's exactly what we recommend during the Design phase. This phase calls for you to brainstorm your Red Goldfish Fry (RGF) around the gaps and opportunities you identified during the Inquire phase.

The goal during the Design phase is to generate as many ideas as possible, whether or not you believe they will be immediately viable. Often the best ideas come from creating a more reasonable or measured version of an idea that's too big, complicated, or expensive to implement.

SET YOUR FOCUS

As we discussed in the previous section, your goal should not be to fill every gap you identified. Instead your goal is to address the gaps that are most damaging to your stakeholder experience. In an ideal world, this will leave budget, time, and other resources to create peak moments for the most promising opportunities.

To this end, your first step in the Design phase is to choose which gaps and opportunities you would like to address. Starting from the list you created, first identify which gaps are the most damaging. Here are some questions you can ask to help you prioritize the list:

After which gaps do we tend to . . .

- lose the most volunteers and donors?

- see NPS (Net Promoter Score) or other measures drop?
- receive the most complaints?

As you ask these questions and rank the gaps accordingly, chances are good that a few will bubble to the top. Those 3-5 top gaps are the ones that should grab your design attention.

We also encourage you to repeat this ranking process for opportunities but use a different set of questions to determine the most promising ones. Here are questions to get started:

Which opportunities . . .

- are directly related to our core service?
- are most important to our target donors?
- will serve the majority of our donors and volunteers?
- will create competitive separation in the marketplace?
- are unlike anything we've done before?

As you can imagine, ranking opportunities is a bit harder. The process requires intuition and will feel more squishy than ranking gaps. This is exactly why so many organizations fall into the trap of only addressing gaps. Our rational brains far prefer the certainty of addressing known gaps to the uncertainty of creating something brand new. Embrace the uncertainty.

Add your 3-5 opportunities to your list of 3-5 gaps. These are your areas of focus for the Design process. You might have completed this ranking alone or with a group. If you worked alone, now is the time to get others involved.

DESIGN PHASE PROGRESS

✓	**Step One:** Set Your Focus
	Step Two: Ask Big Questions
	Step Three: Organize Your Ideas

ASK BIG QUESTIONS

Just before the brainstorming portion of our workshops, we ask participants to complete an exercise. We give each person a blank sheet of paper and ask them to draw a picture of a vase with flowers. Within about 20 seconds, most everyone, regardless of artistic talent, sketches out a container with one or more flowers. We then ask them to draw a second picture. This time, however, we ask them to draw a better way to enjoy flowers in their home. As you might imagine, we receive many different drawings. Often, we go around the room and ask each participant to explain their idea.

We call this a design thinking exercise. Psychologically speaking, it's an example of divergent and convergent thinking. Both terms were coined by psychologist Joy Paul Guilford.

Divergent thinking is a thought process or method used to generate creative ideas by exploring many possible solutions.[85]

Convergent thinking is the opposite of divergent thinking. It generally means the ability to give the "correct" answer to standard questions that do not require significant creativity.[86]

During the exercise, the first prompt—drawing a vase—is a convergent thinking exercise. While some creativity is involved,

---

85. https://en.wikipedia.org/wiki/Divergent_thinking
86. https://en.wikipedia.org/wiki/Convergent_thinking

there is generally one correct answer. The second prompt requires divergent thinking as we're asking participants to come up with a possible solution to the problem and not one correct answer.

You might be wondering what this has to do with designing your Red Goldfish. Everything, in fact. This exercise exists to awaken the parts of our brains that handle divergent thinking. As we start the brainstorming process, we're not looking for the most correct or logical ideas. Rather we are seeking many possible solutions to address the given gap or opportunity.

Harvard Instructor Anne Manning notes that divergent thinking is useful for coming up with ideas and convergent thinking is good for making decisions about those ideas, but it's difficult to do both at the same time.[87] During the Design phase, you and your team should focus on divergent thinking and avoid the temptation to question or evaluate ideas.

We recommend a group brainstorm for generating ideas. There are whole books on the art and science of brainstorming, so we'll just cover our tips for the process.

1. **Environment**. Create an environment for generating new ideas. You might want to consider hosting the brainstorm at an off-site location.

2. **Supplies**. Make sure everyone has what they need to be productive—coffee, water, snacks, and office supplies.

3. **People**. Get the right number of people in the room. Brainstorming works best with 5-8 people. Beyond that number, some participants will mentally check out of the process.

87. https://www.youtube.com/watch?v=xjE2RV6IQzo

4. **Cross-pollination**. In our workshops, participants are often grouped with others from their teams in the organization. This can work well as can intentionally mixing departments to generate different perspectives. We like and use both methods and encourage you to experiment with what works best for you.

5. **Focus and timing**. We recommend focusing on one gap or opportunity at a time. Perhaps even setting a timer or a goal to gather ideas and then moving on to the next gap or opportunity.

6. **Format**. In our workshops, we often ask for individuals to first come up with ideas and then share them with their brainstorming group. Sometimes we use sticky notes to collect all of the individual ideas.

7. **Yes, and**. Remember, the purpose of the exercise is to generate as many ideas as possible, not to evaluate them. You'll want to set strict rules about not dismissing or contradicting any ideas. A helpful way to do that is to start ideas with "yes, and" while avoiding words like "but" and "however" (and other creative phrases to contradict without using these words.)

We called this section "Ask Big Questions" and now that we're set up to brainstorm, we finally get to ask those big questions. We find that it's helpful to ask thought-provoking questions around each gap or opportunity to elicit different ideas to address them. During the brainstorm, your facilitator may choose to ask some of these questions to help elicit ideas.

Here's our go-to list of questions:

- If it were magic, how would it happen?

- If we eliminated X altogether, what could we replace it with?
- What is the confusing part about X?
- How have others solved for X?
- If you had a budget of one million dollars, how would you solve this problem? What about a budget of ten dollars?
- If you had a year to solve this problem, how would you do it? What if you had 10 minutes?

You will likely develop some of your own questions as well. We like questions that go to the extremes as you can see with the last two questions focused on budget and timeline. Oftentimes the best ideas come from the pared back version of a much larger, but infeasible idea. Those questions help develop those big ideas.

As you finish the brainstorming process, make sure you've captured all of your ideas. Taking photos of whiteboards, sticky notes, and flipcharts can be helpful. These will be important reference materials as you move into the next step.

DESIGN PHASE PROGRESS

✓	**Step One:** Set Your Focus
✓	**Step Two:** Ask Big Questions
	Step Three: Organize Your Ideas

ORGANIZE YOUR IDEAS

Now that you've generated many ideas, some of which are likely extraordinary, you'll want to organize them in a uniform way for internal consumption and evaluation. There's no right way to undertake this process, but we do have a few recommendations.

Start by stating the gap or opportunity you're seeking to address. Then, include each idea. For the idea, you'll likely need a short title and a longer description to explain it. This will allow you to talk about the idea before building it out.

Broadly, your ideas will fall into the categories of value and effort. Generally, but not always, ideas to fill gaps will seek to reduce effort and ideas to address opportunities will seek to increase value.

At this stage, you have an organized list of gaps and opportunities along with a list of ideas—the Red Goldfish Fry—that you can now evaluate. Of course, generating ideas is the easy part. Implementation is much harder.

DESIGN PHASE PROGRESS

✓	**Step One:** Set Your Focus
✓	**Step Two:** Ask Big Questions
✓	**Step Three:** Organize Your Ideas

CHAPTER 14

EVALUATE

"Chess masters don't evaluate all the possible moves. They know how to discard 98 percent of the ones they could make and then focus on the best choice of the remaining lot."

— John Dickerson

During the evaluation process, we recommend both internal and external validation. So far most of the Red Goldfish Fry—the ideas—likely came from people inside your organization. Along with the valuable insight each employee or volunteer brought to the idea came the not-so-valuable biases they inherently have.

In the previous chapter we discussed the concepts of divergent and convergent thinking. At this point in the process, we want to reawaken your convergent thinking ability as our objective is no longer to generate ideas but rather to determine analytically the viability of each.

With the list of RGF you generated in the Design phase, you'll now dive into Internal Evaluation.

INTERNAL EVALUATION

Your Internal Evaluation phase starts with the list of RGF you're considering. You'll likely have somewhere between six and ten ideas. You'll want to determine if each of them is likely to work. Since we're not yet involving donors or volunteers, which we'll get to in the next two sections, you'll use this time to evaluate each PGF viability from the organization's perspective.

Is the idea feasible?

Like many of the concepts we discuss, feasibility studies can be quite complex. We recommend that you use your own judgment as to how thorough you would like for your feasibility study to be. If you're a small organization, we recognize that this process might be simple. For a large enterprise, we realize this stage is often where good ideas get stuck. Here are the questions you'll need to answer:

- What resources will be needed to implement this idea?

- What are the costs associated with those resources?
- Do the costs outweigh the benefits?
- If you're successful, how many of your current donors or volunteers are likely to take advantage of this Red Goldfish? Do you expect greater engagement or increased donations of time or money from these stakeholders?
- If you're successful, how many new donors or volunteers do you expect this Red Goldfish may attract?
- Can you expect benefits beyond additional loyalty? Are there any intangible benefits?

It's tempting to think of internal evaluation as an elimination round, but we prefer to think of it as a checkpoint. Instead of looking for reasons to eliminate RGFs from consideration, you're looking for reasons to advance it forward. On the other hand, if you find information that leads you to believe the idea is not viable, you have three options: 1. You can either eliminate the RGF, 2. adjust it to be viable, or 3. wait until after external validation to make a final decision.

In either case, you have now evaluated the feasibility of your RGF. We hope your excitement is growing, because the next step is to start getting input from the most important evaluators—your external stakeholders.

EVALUATE PHASE PROGRESS

✓	**Step One:** Internal Evaluation
	Step Two: External Validation
	Step Three: Pilot

EXTERNAL VALIDATION

At this stage, we advocate for two types of input from your external stakeholders. The first we call validation. The idea behind validation is to use an inexpensive approach for feasibility and avoid the cost of a pilot in the event the idea does not resonate with your audience.

External validation resembles traditional market research. You'll share your ideas with your target audience and receive their feedback. There's no one correct way to accomplish this, but there are plenty of incorrect ways. Here are some of the ways we recommend seeking input from your audience.

- Focus group
- Advisory board meetings
- Surveys
- One-on-one donor and volunteer interviews

No matter which research method you choose, you will want to make sure you do a few things. First, you will want to make sure you describe your idea fully to the volunteer or donor. The title and short description you developed in the Design phase will be helpful, but you may want to include more detail at this stage.

Second, you should get their initial reaction to the idea and then ask if they have any questions about it. First impressions only happen once, so you'll want to capture them immediately.

Third, you'll want to engage further with the volunteers and donors, asking them what they like and dislike about the idea and if implementation of the idea would cause them to engage more with you. Of course, a positive response is not a guarantee as researchers will tell you that humans are bad at predicting their future behavior.

Like many of our recommendations, whole books (and dissertations, for that matter) have been written on market research. You may want to pursue DIY research, or you may want to engage a professional researcher or firm. Engaging a researcher or firm will be more expensive, but it may make sense if you have the budget and the stakes are high. If you choose the DIY route, we encourage you to seek out additional resources on market research to guide you.

Once your research is complete, you will need to make decisions about each one of your RGFs.

As we noted previously, your RFG options are:

1. Eliminate
2. Adjust to be viable
3. Decide based on external validation results

You probably will have a mix of all of the above for your project and that's perfectly okay! It's why we do research before rolling out a pilot project. This research most likely generated some additional insights about your audience that you will want to consider during your pilot, or it may cause you to revisit your journey maps with fresh data.

Jack Welch famously said, "An organization's ability to learn, and translate that learning into action rapidly, is the ultimate competitive advantage." Now that you're armed with customer input, you're ready to start putting your ideas into action.

EVALUATE PHASE PROGRESS

✓	**Step One:** Internal Evaluation
✓	**Step Two:** External Validation
	Step Three: Pilot

PILOT

We're excited you've made it to the pilot stage! There's only so much you can learn from the process we've outlined here. Now you get the privilege of learning directly from your volunteers and donors in a real-world scenario. We are excited for you!

Pilot programs differ depending on the size of the organization and donor/volunteer base. Your pilot may be as simple as trying out one RGF for a day or as complex as rolling out the RGF in a limited number of your locations for a longer period of time. You're the best judge of what will work most effectively for your volunteers and donors.

Here are some tips we recommend you keep in mind as you put together your pilot:

- Make sure your pilot is sufficiently sized by reach and time frame to generate a representative sample of your target audience. Keep in mind that your RGF may be targeting a subset of your donors or volunteers, so you'll want to consider the locations and times when they are most likely to engage.

- Build measurement into the process. As you are planning the pilot, you will want to determine how you'll measure the effects of the RGF. An uptick in donations or new volunteers would be marvelous, but those may be lagging indicators. Consider other ways to measure the response from the pilot audience relative to the rest of your volunteers and donors. Ideally, you would be able to segment the pilot participants from other volunteers and donors to compare multiple metrics.

- Make the experience as real as possible. We suggest not telling the volunteers and donors you are *trying out* something new. Simply say it's something new. In physics, there's a concept called Observer Effect. That is the theory that the mere observation of a phenomenon inevitably changes that phenomenon. We're not physicists, but we do suspect that the knowledge that something is a pilot will change the audience's perception of it.

- Engage in proper training for your team. Remember when outward-facing, it's not a pilot, it's the new thing. You'll want your team to treat the RGF pilot as normally as possible to avoid skewed results or apathy toward the project.

- Listen to your team. To achieve buy-in and an effective launch, you'll also want to seek the feedback of your team members tasked with delivering your new RGF experience. This input will allow you to head off any opposition or issues that might interrupt an effective roll-out.

Once you deploy the RGF pilot and measure its results, you arrive at your final point of analysis—the go or no-go decision. Next, you'll prepare to roll out the RGF that produce desirable results more widely in your organization. It's RGF graduation day for them as they're now Red Goldfish qualified for deployment.

Let's turn our attention now to helping you roll them out successfully!

EVALUATE PHASE PROGRESS

✓	**Step One:** Internal Evaluation
✓	**Step Two:** External Validation
✓	**Step Three:** Pilot

CHAPTER 15

ADVANCE

"The difficulties you meet will resolve themselves as you advance. Proceed, and light will dawn, and shine with increasing clearness on your path."

– Jim Rohn

Welcome to the last step of the I.D.E.A. process—the **Advance** stage. Advancing your newly commissioned Red Goldfish isn't a one-time event. It's a continuous process—one where you seek to advance the Red Goldfish and the overall experience you create for your volunteers and donors to a new level.

During the Advance stage, you have three primary responsibilities:

1. Achieve buy-in internally
2. Roll out the experience to volunteers and donors
3. Set up a feedback loop with continuous measurement

BUY-IN

Every organization operates differently, and your buy-in process will differ accordingly. As a small nonprofit, you may only need to achieve buy-in from a small group. For larger nonprofits, you may have a formal review process and a need to achieve approval from a number of stakeholders. As with considering or implementing any of our advice, you know your organization best, so we're not in a position to be prescriptive about what buy-in you will need to achieve.

We do believe, however, that there are common components of achieving buy-in, so we recommend that you take all of them into account:

- Communicate the plan with the right stakeholders. You'll want to make sure that everyone who has influence over the project is onboard. Don't forget the influence that board members and major donors can wield—involve them as early as possible and ensure you address their concerns.
- Don't forget your front-line staff. These are the people tasked with implementing the Red Goldfish, so their understanding of both why and how to deploy the RGF is essential.

- Present the story of the idea. It might be tempting to say, "We decided to do this, and these are the results." While that is true, a significant amount of work went into formulating the RGF throughout the Inquire, Design, and Evaluate phases. Make sure everyone knows how the Red Goldfish came to be.

- Use anecdotes to win hearts. During the pilot, you no doubt heard anecdotal feedback of how the Red Goldfish helped a beneficiary. By sharing some of that feedback, you will connect with and engender empathy (and usually support) from your stakeholders.

- Use data to win minds. Thinking back to the discussion about convergent thinking, you know you'll need numbers to prove that the Red Goldfish was successful. You gathered significant data from the pilot, so use it to share (and prove) what you learned.

- Present adjustments based on pilot feedback. A story where everything is perfect not only isn't believable, it's boring. You'll want to present some of the learnings from the pilot as well as the adjustments they necessitated to solidify buy-in.

We can't guarantee an easy buy-in process if you follow these tips, but we can guarantee that you'll set yourself up for success. Once you achieve buy-in, the most fun part comes next—rolling out your Red Goldfish to your volunteers and donors!

ADVANCE PHASE PROGRESS

✓	**Step One:** Buy-In
	Step Two: Rollout
	Step Three: Measurement

ROLLOUT

Let's do this! Rollout is one of the most exciting and critical parts of the journey. You'll soon see the fruits of your labor, but to do so, you'll need a successful roll out. Just as in each of the previous phases, how you roll out your Red Goldfish will be based on your organization, the resources involved, and any number of other factors. Much as before, this leaves us to offer our generalized guidance. We encourage you to adapt as necessary to suit your needs.

Here are some of the factors you should consider during roll out.

- Communication – How will you communicate the Red Goldfish offering to both front-line employees and volunteers and donors?
- Policies – How clear are your policies for what's allowed and disallowed? Have you considered edge cases or exceptions?
- Logistics – What new materials need to be acquired and distributed to the front-line?
- Metrics – How will you collect relevant metrics? You measured during the pilot, so you already have a start. How will standard measurement differ from the pilot?
- Promotion – We don't advocate for Red Goldfish as a PR strategy, but you may need to promote the offering to gain initial usage by the target audience.

Rollout may seem simple, however, it is anything but. How well you roll out your Red Goldfish may determine its fate. This time might be marked by late nights and early mornings, but all of the work you've done up to this point should provide the necessary motivation to make it happen. We believe in you (and your Red Goldfish)!

ADVANCE PHASE PROGRESS

✓	Step One: Buy-In
✓	Step Two: Rollout
	Step Three: Measurement

MEASUREMENT

As you know from the pilot, measurement is how you prove your Red Goldfish is working and delivering the desired results for the organization. Measurement is also how you gain valuable insights that will help you return to the Inquire phase and address new (or different) gaps and opportunities. Here are some of our tips for effective measurement, realizing, as you know by now, that every organization is different.

- Be sure to collect performance data. You identified the metrics as a part of the roll out, so now you'll want to collect and analyze the data.

- Use segmentation to understand relative performance. Over time, the enthusiastic buy-in you achieved may wane, so you'll want to show how the Red Goldfish consistently delivers results. Ideally, you will be able to compare key metrics between those customers who experience the Red Goldfish and those who did not.

- Mind the bottom line. You'll want to connect the performance of the Red Goldfish to metrics as close to the bottom line as possible. By showing increased donor retention, volunteer time, and board engagement because of the Red Goldfish, you're likely to retain the necessary support to keep the goldfish swimming. (No apologies for the pun.)

- Refine as needed. There's no reason you can't tweak as you go along. Despite the best planning and analysis, your Red Goldfish may miss the mark slightly. Don't hesitate to make adjustments as needed but resist the urge to make them too early. There's no right answer here, so follow your gut. It's usually right.

- Build the feedback loop. Continue collecting the necessary data to loop back to the Inquire phase. As you improve, the desire to improve will grow in your organization. Use this desire, your new data, and, hopefully, your new results to fuel the feedback loop. This will create a flywheel effect that allows your organization to reach new heights on a continuous basis.

Woohoo! You've made it through the I.D.E.A. Process! Our excitement level is high, because we know that with every Red Goldfish out in the wild, there's a donor or volunteer somewhere whose experience is just a little better than it was before. It's why we do what we do, and we hope you share the same excitement.

ADVANCE PHASE PROGRESS

✓	**Step One:** Buy-In
✓	**Step Two:** Rollout
✓	**Step Three:** Measurement

WHAT HAPPENS NEXT?

Your goal is to consistently move to the next plateau on each iteration through the I.D.E.A. Process. As we've said, a Red Goldfish isn't a campaign—it's a commitment. What was once a differentiator can quickly become an expectation, so consistent improvement is essential in today's hyper-competitive marketplace. New successes come with increased expectations which bring up new issues. It's not just about a completing the I.D.E.A. Process again, it's about consistently serving the volunteers and donors.

FIVE TOP TAKEAWAYS

"Advice is like a tablet of aspirin.
It tends to only work if you take it."

– David Murphy

Here are the top five takeaways from Red Goldfish Nonprofit Edition:

1. A purpose-first mindset, fueled by the rising number of nonprofits and mission-driven organizations, is changing the way we work and do business for the foreseeable future. It is our belief that during the next decade there will no longer be a large distinction between for-profit companies and nonprofit organizations. The evolution of corporate social responsibility, benefit corporations, new nonprofit models, and the conscious capitalism movement have forever blurred the line of how we look at organizations. Nonprofits no longer are alone in pursuing the greater good. Business is changing.

2. Nonprofits that have a strong, defined purpose find that it drives staff engagement, connects with volunteers, and fuels donations. An emerging view of a nonprofit is putting purpose at the center of everything, followed by staff, volunteers, and donors.

3. You can't have happy enthused volunteers and donors if you don't have happy engaged staff. Beyond basic compensation,

it is important to do the little things to reinforce purpose and drive engagement for team members.

4. When it comes to donor engagement and understanding what is important to making initial and repeating gifts, three key factors emerge: creative communication, leveraging technology, and providing incentives.

5. There is a four-step I.D.E.A. process for designing improvements for your nonprofit:

Inquire – understand what is important to your stakeholders and what gaps and opportunities exist in their journey.

Design – generate ideas for Red Goldfish to address the gaps and opportunities in your current customer journey.

Evaluate – complete internal analysis and external pilot to determine which Red Goldfish, or RGF (Red Goldfish Fry) for short, should be rolled out across the organization.

Advance – bring your best RGFs out of the pilot phase and into widespread rollout, measuring the results, and creating a feedback loop back to the Inquire phase.

ABOUT THE AUTHORS

STAN PHELPS, CSP

Stan Phelps is a best-selling author, keynote speaker, and workshop facilitator. He believes that today's organizations must focus on meaningful differentiation to win the hearts of both employees and customers.

He is the founder of PurpleGoldfish.com. Purple Goldfish is a think tank of customer experience and employee engagement experts that offers keynotes and workshops that drive loyalty and sales. The group helps organizations connect with the hearts and minds of customers and employees.

Prior to PurpleGoldfish.com, Stan had a 20-year career in marketing that included leadership positions at IMG, adidas, PGA Exhibitions, and Synergy. At Synergy, he worked on award-winning experiential programs for top brands such as KFC, Wachovia, NASCAR, Starbucks, and M&M's.

It should read, Stan is a TEDx speaker, a Forbes contributor, and Certified Speaking Professional. He has spoken at over 400 events across Australia, Bahrain, Canada, Ecuador, France, Germany, Holland, Israel, Japan, Malaysia, Peru, Russia, Singapore, Spain, Sweden, UK, Vietnam, and the US.

He is the author of ten other business books and one fun one:

- Purple Goldfish 2.0 – 10 Ways to Attract Raving Customers
- Green Goldfish 2.0 - 15 Keys to Driving Employee Engagement

- Golden Goldfish - The Vital Few
- Blue Goldfish - Using Technology, Data, and Analytics to Drive Both Profits and Prophets
- Purple Goldfish Service Edition - 12 Ways Hotels, Restaurants, and Airlines Win the Right Customers
- Red Goldfish - Motivating Sales and Loyalty Through Shared Passion and Purpose
- Pink Goldfish - Defy Ordinary, Exploit Imperfection, and Captivate Your Customers
- Purple Goldfish Franchise Edition - The Ultimate S.Y.S.T.E.M. for Franchisors and Franchisees
- Yellow Goldfish - Nine Ways to Drive Happiness in Business for Growth, Productivity, and Prosperity
- Gray Goldfish – Navigating the Gray Areas to Successfully Lead Every Generation
- Bar Tricks, Bad Jokes, & Even Worse Stories

Stan received a BS in Marketing and Human Resources from Marist College, a JD/MBA from Villanova University, and a certificate for Achieving Breakthrough Service from Harvard Business School. He is a Certified Net Promoter Associate and has taught as an adjunct professor at NYU, Rutgers University, and Manhattanville College. Stan is also a fellow at Maddock Douglas, an innovation consulting firm in Chicago. Stan lives in Cary, North Carolina, with his wife, Jennifer, and two boys, Thomas and James.

To book Stan for an upcoming keynote, webinar, or workshop go to stanphelpsspeaks.com. You can reach Stan at stan@purplegoldfish.com or call +1.919.360.4702 or follow him on Twitter: @StanPhelpsPG.

KEITH GREEN

Keith Green is an Assistant Professor of Public Relations and Strategic Communication at Montclair State University. He is the principal at Emerald Owl Communications, a strategic communications consultancy that specializes in creating PR campaigns, driving earned media, conceptualizing experiential marketing programs, and generating new business for brands and agencies.

He leverages his experience at the Philadelphia 76ers, Richmond Raceway, Synergy Events, and Guinness World Records to bring creative solutions to life for his clients.

In 2015, Keith expanded his PR, marketing, community relations, and sales experience to include the role of a nonprofit founder and leader when he formed the Autism MVP Foundation. The all-volunteer nonprofit was inspired by Keith's son and the educators and therapists who have helped make a difference in the life of Keith's family. The organization is dedicated to increasing the number of autism-focused educators. The foundation's programs include a groundbreaking training program for teachers and paraprofessionals and a scholarship initiative for graduate students who are committed to pursuing a career to improve educational, social, and life skill outcomes for individuals who have autism. Both programs are currently affiliated with Monmouth University.

His experience working with universities also includes more than 10 years of experience as an adjunct faculty member. He has taught sports PR and marketing classes to graduate and undergraduate students at Virginia Commonwealth University, Virginia State University, Utah Valley University, and University of Phoenix.

Keith is a proud two-time graduate of Temple University where he sharpened his writing skills as an undergraduate journalism major. Three years after graduating and while working full-time for the Philadelphia 76ers, he returned to Temple and earned his M.Ed. in sports administration and recreation.

Keith lives in New Jersey with his wife, Donna, and their son, Gavin. When he's not cheering on his favorite Philadelphia sport teams, including his beloved Temple Owls, he can be found playing golf, cooking, and spending time with his family on the New Jersey beaches.

To book Keith for an upcoming keynote, webinar, or workshop, you can reach him at keith@emeraldowlcomms.com or 732-870-7977. You can also connect with him on LinkedIn at www.linkedin.com/in/keithagreen or on Twitter @EmeraldOwlComms or @KeithsTweets.

OTHER COLORS IN THE GOLDFISH SERIES

Purple Goldfish 2.0 – 12 Ways to Attract Raving Customers. This book is based on the Purple Goldfish Project, a crowdsourcing effort that collected more than 1,001 examples of signature-added value. The book draws inspiration from the concept of lagniappe, providing 10 practical strategies for winning the hearts of customers and influencing positive word of mouth.

Green Goldfish 2.0 – 15 Keys to Driving Employee Engagement. Green Goldfish is based on the simple premise that "happy engaged employees create happy enthused customers." The book focuses on 15 different ways to drive employee engagement and reinforce a strong corporate culture.

Golden Goldfish – The Vital Few: All Customers and Employees Are Not Created Equal. Golden Goldfish examines the importance of your top 20 percent of customers and employees. The book showcases nine ways to drive loyalty and retention with these two critical groups.

Blue Goldfish - Using Technology, Data, and Analytics to Drive Both Profits and Prophets. Blue Goldfish examines how to leverage technology, data, and analytics to do a "little something extra" to improve the experience for the customer. The book is based on a collection of over 300 case studies. It examines the three R's: Relationship, Responsiveness, and Readiness. *Blue Goldfish* also uncovers eight different ways to turn insights into action.

Red Goldfish - Motivating Sales and Loyalty Through Shared Passion and Purpose. Purpose is changing the way we work and how customers choose business partners. It is driving loyalty, and it's on its way to becoming the ultimate differentiator in business. *Red Goldfish* shares cutting edge examples and reveals the eight ways businesses can embrace purpose that drives employee engagement, fuels the bottom line, and makes an impact on the lives of those it serves.

Purple Goldfish Service Edition - 12 Ways Hotels, Restaurants, and Airlines Win the Right Customers. Purple Goldfish Service Edition is about differentiation via added value and marketing to your existing customers via G.L.U.E. (giving little unexpected extras). Packed with over 100 examples, the book focuses on the 12 ways to do the "little extras" to improve the customer experience for restaurants, hotels, and airlines. The end result is increased sales, happier customers, and positive word of mouth.

Pink Goldfish - Defy Normal, Exploit Imperfection, and Captivate Your Customers. Companies need to stand out in a crowded marketplace, but true differentiation is increasingly rare. Based on over 200 case studies, *Pink Goldfish* provides an unconventional seven-part framework for achieving competitive separation by embracing flaws instead of fixing them.

Purple Goldfish Franchise Edition - The Ultimate S.Y.S.T.E.M. For Franchisors and Franchisees. Packed with over 100 best-practice examples, *Purple Goldfish Franchise Edition* focuses on the six keys to creating a successful franchise S.Y.S.T.E.M. and a dozen ways to create a signature customer experience.

Yellow Goldfish - Nine Ways to Drive Happiness in Business for Growth, Productivity, and Prosperity. There should only be one success metric in business and that's happiness. A Yellow Goldfish is any time a business does a little extra to contribute to the happiness of its customers, employees, or society. Based on nearly 300 case studies,

Yellow Goldfish provides a nine-part framework for happiness-driven growth, productivity, and prosperity in business.

Gray Goldfish – Navigating the Gray Areas to Successfully Lead Every Generation. How do you successfully lead the five generations in today's workforce? You need to know how to navigate successfully. Filled with over 100 case studies and the Generational Matrix, *Gray Goldfish* provides the definitive map for leaders to follow as they recruit, train, manage, and inspire across the generations.

Made in the USA
Lexington, KY
26 November 2019